RESTRICTED

OFFICE OF THE
ASSISTANT CHIEF OF AIR STAFF, INTELLIGENCE
WASHINGTON, D. C.

Italian Aircraft and Armament

INFORMATIONAL INTELLIGENCE

SUMMARY No. 43–39

July 1943

Distribution: SQUADRONS

NOT TO BE TAKEN INTO THE AIR
ON COMBAT MISSIONS

RESTRICTED

The Naval & Military Press Ltd

Published by

The Naval & Military Press Ltd
Unit 5 Riverside, Brambleside
Bellbrook Industrial Estate
Uckfield, East Sussex
TN22 1QQ England

Tel: +44 (0)1825 749494

www.naval-military-press.com
www.nmarchive.com

In reprinting in facsimile from the original, any imperfections are inevitably reproduced and the quality may fall short of modern type and cartographic standards.

OFFICE OF THE
ASSISTANT CHIEF OF THE AIR STAFF, INTELLIGENCE
WASHINGTON, D. C.

Distribution: SQUADRONS. July 1943

ITALIAN AIRCRAFT AND ARMAMENT

Introduction

This booklet is compiled to present in tabular form technical information at present available concerning currently operational types of Italian aircraft, together with the armament they carry. In addition, the best available photographs and silhouettes are shown, approximate fields of fire being indicated on the latter. A brief description of each aircraft is given.

A standard form is used to describe the technical data as now known. Supplementary information will be disseminated in Informational Intelligence Summaries, under the heading "Notes On Enemy Aircraft". This additional data should be transcribed into this Summary, either on the current sheets or on the blank forms at the end of each classification.

Individual aircraft are classified according to general use and are arranged in alphabetical and numerical order in each group. By numbering sheets in allotments of 100 to each group, provision is made for adding newly recorded types at the end of their proper classification in the general index.

Information has been obtained from sources believed reliable, but is incomplete in the case of certain aircraft. Further data on all aircraft are urgently desired, particularly with reference to new or unfamiliar models.

THE AIRCRAFT SHOWN ON THE FRONT COVER IS THE MC 202

INDEX

FIGHTERS

		Sheet No.
FIAT	CR 42	101
FIAT	G 50	102
MACCHI	MC 200	103
MACCHI	MC 202	104
MACCHI	MC 205	105
REGGIANE	RE 2000	106
REGGIANE	RE 2001	107

BOMBERS, GROUND ATTACK, RECONNAISSANCE

BREDA	BA 88	201
FIAT	BR 20M	202
CAPRONI	CA 135 bis	203
CAPRONI	CA 310	204
CAPRONI	CA 311, 312 bis	205
CAPRONI	CA 313	206
CANTIERI RIUNITI	CANT Z 1007 bis	207
FIAT	CR 25	208
PIAGGIO	P 108	209
SAVOIA-MARCHETTI	SM 79	210
SAVOIA-MARCHETTI	SM 84 bis	211

ARMY COOPERATION, BOMBER-TRANSPORTS

FIAT	G 12	301
MERIDIONALI	RO 37 bis	302
SAVOIA-MARCHETTI	SM 75	303
SAVOIA-MARCHETTI	SM 81	304
SAVOIA-MARCHETTI	SM 82	305

MARINE AIRCRAFT

CAPRONI	CA 312 bis, I. S.	401
CAPRONI	CA 316	402
CANTIERI RIUNITI	CANT Z 501	403
CANTIERI RIUNITI	CANT Z 506B	404
MERIDIONALI	RO 43	405
MERIDIONALI	RO 44	406
FIAT	RS 14	407

RESTRICTED

CALCULATION OF RANGES

*I. (a) The method of assessing the ranges is based on the following conventions:—
  (i) Ranges given are ideal still-air ranges. No reduction is made for operational tactics or allowance made for navigational errors, head winds, etc.
  (ii) Allowance is made for warming up and take off equivalent to five minutes running at take-off power.
  (iii) A further allowance is made for the fuel used during climb to the operational altitude at the maximum rate of climb.
  (iv) The distance covered during the climb is credited to the range but no credit is given for gliding in at the end of the journey.

The actual values of these allowances are not given in the tables, which are laid out to give the available data in as concise a manner as possible.

(b) Figures are, however, given at each loading condition for the average rate of fuel consumption, expressed in miles per 100 lb. of fuel. These will enable approximate estimates to be made of the effect on range and endurance of interchanging fuel with other loads (e. g. bombs). For example, supposing the following data are given:—

	Fuel			Normal cruising			
Bombs	Gals.	Lbs.	Average speed m. p. h.	Altitude ft.	Range miles	Endurance hrs.	Miles per 100 lb.
Nil	88	670	315	16,500	450	1.48	80

and it is required to calculate the resulting range and endurance when some form of additional load weighing 150 lb. is carried at the expense of fuel.

Range.—150 lb. is 1.5 times a 100 lb. unit, and the consequent reduction in range would be 1.5 times the "miles per 100 lb." figure, i. e. 80 in this case, which would be 120 miles, and this subtracted from the range figure, i. e. 450 miles, would give an amended range of 330 miles.

Endurance.—The resulting reduction in endurance will be the loss of range divided by the corresponding speed. In this case 120 miles should be divided by the speed in question, i. e. 315 mph which gives .38 hour, and, subtracted from the endurance of 1.48 hours, modifies the flying time to 1.1 hours.

It should be noted that these results are very approximate as further corrections have to be made if changes in the all-up weight, or the over-all drag of the aircraft are involved. They will, however, be sufficiently accurate for most purposes.

*II. Figures will be given, where practicable, under "Remarks" for the fuel consumed by fighters during quarter or half an hour's running at maximum power for combat, but this figure, as stated in Note 1, will not have been deducted from the range figures given.

It will, however, enable estimates of range to be made when it is required to allow for time for combat. For instance, in the example of para. 1 (b) supposing half an hour's combat allowance is given as 290 lb. and it is desired to know the reduction in range in endurance allowing 20 minutes for combat.

Combat allowance.—The fuel consumed would be $^{20}/_{30}$ of 290 lb. which is about 195 lb. which, multiplied by the figure for "miles per 100 lb." i. e. 80, would give a reduction in range of 155 miles, or, as before, if divided by the corresponding speed, i. e. 315 mph gives a reduction in endurance equivalent to about .5 hours off the 1.48 hours listed.

ITALY	CR 42	JULY
101		1943

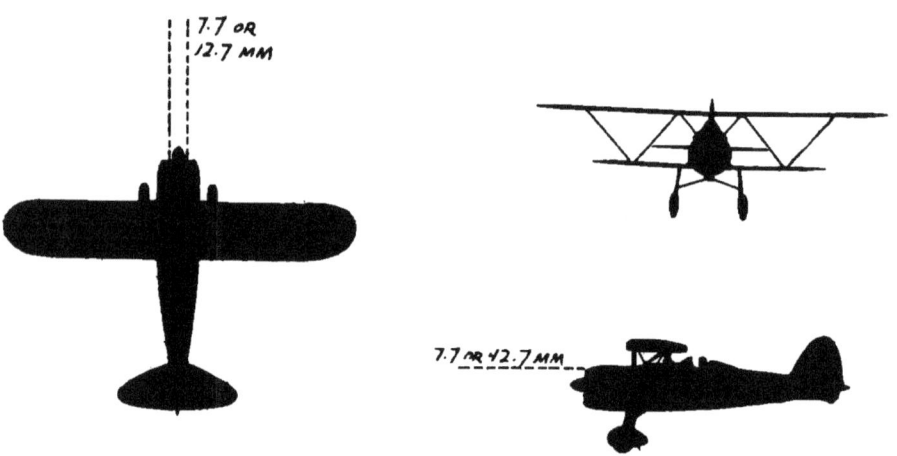

CR 42

DESCRIPTION

The CR 42 is an obsolete day fighter that has been converted into a ground attack and night fighting aircraft. It is the only recognized night fighter in the I.A.F. "CR" stands for "Caccia Rosatelli," fighter designed by Rosatelli.

This aircraft is a single-engine biplane. Wings are of unequal span, the top being the longer. Ailerons are on the top wing only. Warren girder interplane bracing is employed. Forward fuselage is triangular-shaped, fairing to oval section in the rear. The cockpit is open. There is a single fin and rudder. The braced landing gear is fixed. Wheels are spatted.

JULY 1943		ITALY
	CR 42	101

SINGLE-ENGINE FIGHTER.

Mfr.: **FIAT.**   Crew: **ONE.**

Duty: **GROUND ATTACK. NIGHT FIGHTER. BOMBING.**

PERFORMANCE

Max. speed __270__ m.p.h. at __13,100__ ft. altitude (normal load); 260 mph (with max. bombs).

Cruising speed: normal __232__ m.p.h.; economical __150__ m.p.h.; at __13,100__ ft. altitude.

Climb: to __13,000__ ft. altitude in __5.5__ min. (normal load); in 6 min. (with max. bombs).

Fuel: normal __93__ U.S. gals.; max. __115__ U.S. gals. For ½ hr. combat: 40 gals.

Service ceiling: normal load __32,000__ ft.; max. bomb/fuel load __30,500__ ft.; min. fuel/no bombs __34,000__ ft.

RANGES

Speeds	With Normal Fuel/Bomb Load	With Max. Bomb Load	With Max. Fuel Load
Normal cruising	425 miles	400 miles	miles
Economical cruising	575 miles	535 miles	miles

POWER PLANT

Number of motors __1__   Rated __840__ horsepower each at __12,500__ ft. altitude.

Description: **Fiat A.74 RC.38, 14 cyl., twin-row, air-cooled radial.**

Propellers: **3-blade, constant speed, Fiat Hamilton.**

Superchargers: _____

Misc.: **Long chord cowling with controllable gills.**

ARMAMENT

(F - fixed. M - free.)

For'd fuselage: 1 x 7.7 mm and 1/2 x 12.7mm (F)
For'd wings: _____
Through hub: _____
Dorsal: _____
Lateral: _____
Ventral: _____
Tail: _____

BOMB/FREIGHT LOAD

Normal bomb load: _____ lbs.
Max. bomb load: 220 lbs.
Typical bomb stowage: _____

Alternate bomb stowage: _____ lbs.

2 x 110 lbs.
1 x 220 lbs.

Freight and/or troops: _____ lbs.

ARMOR

Frontal: _____
Windshield: _____
Pilot's seat: **Fully protected**
Dorsal: _____
Lateral: _____
Ventral: _____
Bulkhead: _____
Self-sealing fuel tanks, 14 mm. thick.
Engine: _____

SPECIFICATIONS

Materials: **Steel tubing, fabric and metal covering.**

Span: __31'-10"__   Length: __27'-2"__   Height: __10'__   Wing Area (gross) 237 sq.ft.

Weights: landing __4,500__ lbs.; normal load __5,100__ lbs.; max. load (est.) __5,300__ lbs.

Misc.: **Self-sealing covering, 14 mm. thick, on fuel tanks included 2½ mm. pressed felt as the innermost layer, as well as sponge rubber, rubber sheet and doped fabric.**

ADDITIONAL TECHNICAL DATA

Fiat A.76 R.C.40 engine, rated at 1000 hp at 13,100 ft. reported fitted in an improved version.

| ITALY 102 | G 50 | JULY 1943 |

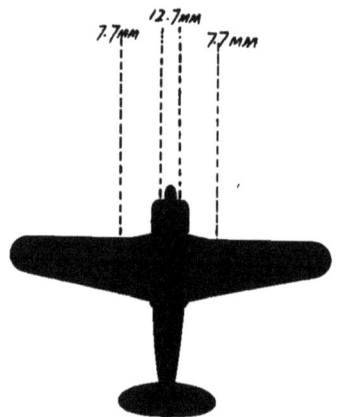

G 50

DESCRIPTION

The G 50 was the first monoplane fighter adopted by the I.A.F. It is obsolescent in terms of modern fighters and probably will be employed mostly for ground-attack operations. "G" stands for Gabrielli, the designer.

This aircraft is a single-engine, low-wing monoplane. Wing center section tapers more sharply in chord and thickness than outer sections, which have moderate taper to rounded tips. Frise ailerons and camber-changing flaps are fitted; ailerons and flap controls are interconnected. The forward fuselage is of oval section; the rear portion straight-sided with an inverted "V" top. There is a single fin and rudder. Current type has open cockpit with head fairing. Landing gear retracts inward into recesses below fuselage and center section.

JULY 1943 — G 50 — ITALY 102

SINGLE-ENGINE FIGHTER

Mfr.: **FIAT** Crew: **ONE**
Duty: **FIGHTING, GROUND ATTACK.**

PERFORMANCE

Max. speed **300** m.p.h. at **14,500** ft. altitude; 260 mph at sea level.
Cruising speed: normal **258** m.p.h.; economical **170** m.p.h.; at **14,500** ft. altitude.
Climb: to **15,000** ft. altitude in **6.4** min. (normal load); in 6.9 min. (with max. load).
Fuel: normal **69** U.S. gals.; max. **83** U.S. gals. For ½ hr. combat: **40** gals.
Service ceiling: normal load **32,500** ft.; max. bomb/fuel load **31,500** ft.; min. fuel/no bombs **34,000** ft.

RANGES

Speeds	With Normal Fuel/Bomb Load	With Max. Bomb Load	With Max. Fuel Load
Normal cruising	325 miles	250 miles	410 miles
Economical cruising	410 miles	320 miles	510 miles

POWER PLANT

Number of motors **1** Rated **840** horsepower each at **12,500** ft. altitude.
Description: **Fiat A.74 RC.38, 14 cyl., twin-row, air-cooled radial.**
Propellers: **3-blade, constant speed, Fiat Hamilton.**
Superchargers:
Misc.: **Long-chord cowling with controllable gills. Air intake under cowling.**

ARMAMENT

(F - fixed. M - free.)
For'd fuselage: **2 x 12.7 mm (F)**
For'd wings: **Provision for 2 x 7.7 mm (F)**
Through hub:
Dorsal:
Lateral:
Ventral:
Tail:

BOMB/FREIGHT LOAD

Normal bomb load: ___ lbs.
Max. bomb load: **317** lbs.
Typical bomb stowage: ___ lbs.
Alternate bomb stowage: ___ lbs.
Freight and/or troops: ___ lbs.

ARMOR

Frontal:
Windshield:
Pilot's seat: **Back, 8 mm., Sides and seat, 6 mm.**
Dorsal:
Lateral:
Ventral:
Bulkhead:
Engine:

SPECIFICATIONS

Materials: **Steel tubing, stressed skin, duralumin spars and ribs.**
Span: **35'-9"** Length: **25'-6"** Height: **9'-3"** Wing Area (gross) **196** sq.ft.
Weights: landing **4,800** lbs.; normal load **5,200** lbs.; max. load (est.) **5,450** lbs.
Misc.: **Two self-sealing fuel tanks behind engine.**

ADDITIONAL TECHNICAL DATA

Fiat A.76 RC.40 engine, rated at 1000 hp at 13,100 ft., reported to be fitted in improved version, which would increase performance.

ITALY	MC 200	JULY
103		1943

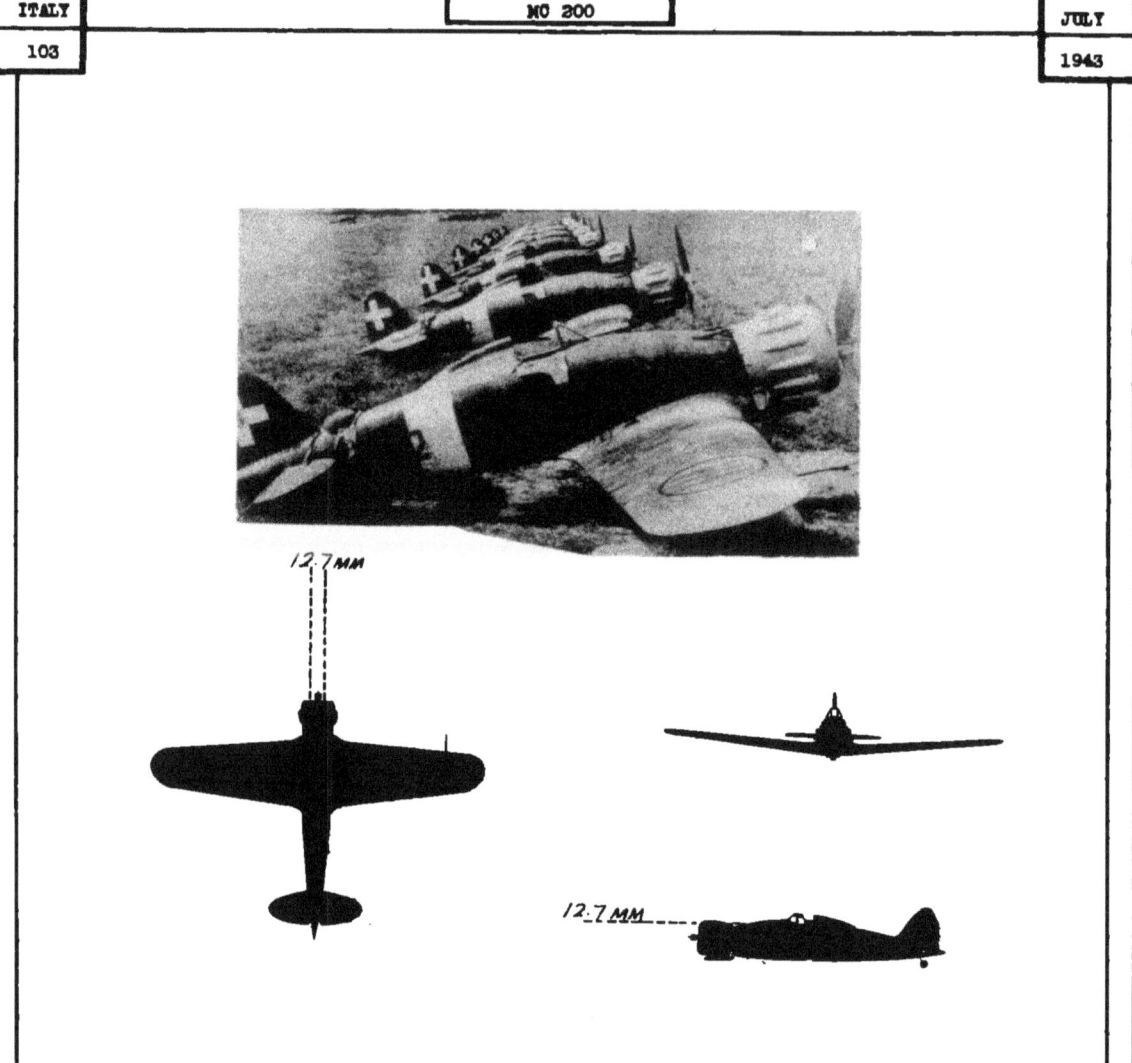

MC 200

DESCRIPTION

The MC 200 is a fighter which has been replaced for the most part by MC 202's and Reggiane 2001's. It will probably see service in the future mainly as a ground attack and light bombing aircraft. "MC" denotes Macchi, designed by Castoldi.

This aircraft is a single-engine, low-wing monoplane. Wings are tapered moderately. Camber-changing flaps are interconnected with the ailerons. Fuselage is of oval section. The cockpit on the current type is closed. Landing gear retracts inward into center section.

| JULY 1943 | MC 200 | ITALY 103 |

SINGLE-ENGINE FIGHTER

Mfr.: **MACCHI**   Crew: **ONE**

Duty: **FIGHTING. GROUND ATTACK. BOMBING.**

PERFORMANCE

Max. speed **310** m.p.h. at **15,000** ft. altitude; **268** mph at sea level.

Cruising speed: normal **268** m.p.h.; economical **170** m.p.h.; at **15,000** ft. altitude.

Climb: to **15,000** ft. altitude in **6.25** min.

Fuel: normal **84** U.S. gals.; max. **163** U.S. gals. For ½ hr. combat: **40** gals.

Service ceiling: normal load **33,000** ft.; max. bomb/fuel load _____ ft.; min. fuel/no bombs **33,500** ft.

RANGES

Speeds	With Normal Fuel/Bomb Load	With Max. Bomb Load	With Max. Fuel Load
Normal cruising	430 miles	miles	miles
Economical cruising	570 miles	miles	900 miles

POWER PLANT

Number of motors **1**   Rated **840** horsepower each at **12,500** ft. altitude.

Description: **Fiat A.74 RC.38, 14 cyl., twin-row, air-cooled radial.**

Propellers: **3-blade, metal, constant speed, Fiat-Hamilton or Piaggio.**

Superchargers:

Misc.: **Long chord cowling with prominent streamlined fairings for rocker boxes. Air intake under cowling.**

ARMAMENT

(F - fixed. M - free.)

For'd fuselage: **2 x 12.7 mm(F)**
For'd wings:
Through hub:
Dorsal:
Lateral:
Ventral:
Tail:

BOMB/FREIGHT LOAD

Normal bomb load: (est.) **220** lbs.
Max. bomb load: _____ lbs.
Typical bomb stowage:
1 light bomb carrier
under each wing   **2 x 110** lbs.
Alternate bomb stowage:
_____ lbs.
Freight and/or troops: _____ lbs.

ARMOR

Frontal:
Windshield:
Pilot's seat: **Back, 8mm.**
sides and back, 6 mm.
Dorsal:
Lateral:
Ventral:
Bulkhead:
Engine:

SPECIFICATIONS

Materials: **All metal, stressed skin.**

Span: **35'**   Length: **27'**   Height: **11'-6"**   Wing Area (gross) **181** sq.ft.

Weights: landing **4,400** lbs.; normal load **5,440** lbs.; max. load _____ lbs.

Misc.:

ADDITIONAL TECHNICAL DATA

Fiat A.76 RC.40 engine, rated at 1000 hp at 1000 hp at 13,100 ft. reported fitted in improved version, which would increase performance.

ITALY	MC 202	JULY
104		1943

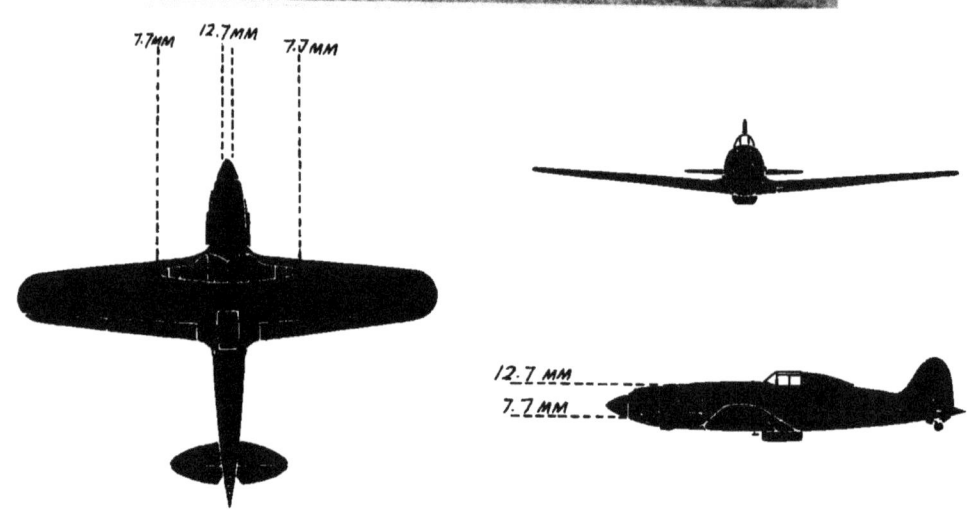

MC 202

DESCRIPTION

The MC 202 is one of the best fighters of the I.A.F. It has been used extensively and forms the backbone of Italian fighter opposition.

This aircraft is a single-engine, low-wing monoplane. Wings taper moderately to rounded tips. Camber-changing flaps are interconnected with the ailerons. The stabilizer is adjustable. Cockpit is over the trailing edge with head fairing extending to rear and merging with fuselage. Landing gear retracts hydraulically inward into center section.

JULY 1943 | MC 202 | ITALY 104

SINGLE-ENGINE FIGHTER

Mfr.: MACCHI. Crew: ONE.
Duty: FIGHTING. GROUND ATTACK. POSSIBLY BOMBING.

PERFORMANCE

Max. speed __360__ m.p.h. at __20,000__ ft. altitude; 295 mph at sea level.

Cruising speed: normal __310__ m.p.h.; economical __195__ m.p.h.; at __18,000__ ft. altitude.

Climb: to __18,000__ ft. altitude in __7.2__ min.

Fuel: normal __106__ U.S. gals.; max. _____ U.S. gals. Fuel for ¼ hr. combat: 47 gals.

Service ceiling: normal load __35,000__ ft.; max. bomb/fuel load _____ ft.; min. fuel/no bombs __36,000__ ft.

RANGES

Speeds	With Normal Fuel/Bomb Load	With Max. Bomb Load	With Max. Fuel Load
Normal cruising	425 miles	miles	miles
Economical cruising	550 miles	miles	miles

POWER PLANT

Number of motors __1__ Rated __1150__ horsepower each at __16,000__ ft. altitude.

Description: DB 601 A/A/1, 12 cyl., liquid-cooled, inverted "V".

Propellers: 3-blade, metal, variable pitch.

Superchargers: Long tunnel intake, air cleaner embodied.

Misc.: Engine made sometimes in Italy under license. Rearward facing exhaust stubs.
Oil cooler under engine, coolant radiator under cockpit.

ARMAMENT

(F - fixed. M - free.)

For'd fuselage: 2 x 12.7 mm (F)
350 r.p.g.
For'd wings: Provision for 2 x 7.7 mm. (F)
Through hub:
Dorsal:
Lateral:
Ventral:
Tail:

BOMB/FREIGHT LOAD

Normal bomb load: _____ lbs.
Max. bomb load: __440__ lbs.
Typical bomb stowage:

Alternate bomb stowage: 2 x 220 lbs.

Freight and/or troops: _____ lbs.
_____ lbs.

ARMOR

Frontal:
Windshield: 2" b.p. glass
Pilot's seat: Back, 8 mm.
Head, 8 mm.
Dorsal:
Lateral:
Ventral:
Bulkhead:
Engine:

SPECIFICATIONS

Materials: All metal, stressed skin.

Span: __34'-8"__ Length: __29'-1"__ Height: __11'-6"__ Wing Area: (gross) 181 sq.ft.

Weights: landing __5,700__ lbs.; normal load __6,400__ lbs.; max. load _____ lbs.

Misc.: Self-sealing tanks behind and under pilot.

ADDITIONAL TECHNICAL DATA

ITALY	MC 205	JULY
105		1943

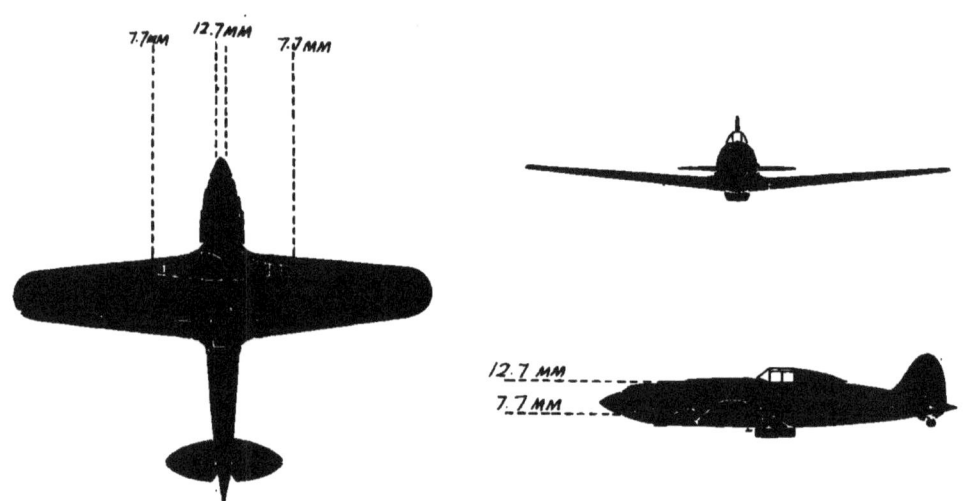

MC 205

DESCRIPTION

The MC 205 appears to be the MC 202 fitted with the more powerful D.B.605A engine. It is probable that the number of these aircraft in service is limited at present.

From an identification point of view, the MC 205 is practically the same as the MC 202 shown on page 104.

JULY		ITALY
1943	MC 205	105

SINGLE-ENGINE FIGHTER

Mfr.: MACCHI.   Crew: ONE.
Duty: FIGHTING. GROUND ATTACK.

PERFORMANCE

Max. speed 385 m.p.h. at 22,000 ft. altitude.

Cruising speed: normal _____ m.p.h.; economical _____ m.p.h.; at _____ ft. altitude.

Climb: to _____ ft. altitude in _____ min.

Fuel: normal 106 U.S. gals.; max. _____ U.S. gals.

Service ceiling: normal load 35,000 ft.; max. bomb/fuel load _____ ft.; min. fuel/no bombs _____ ft.

RANGES

Speeds	With Normal Fuel/Bomb Load	With Max. Bomb Load	With Max. Fuel Load
Normal cruising	400 miles	_____ miles	_____ miles
Economical cruising	580 miles	_____ miles	_____ miles

POWER PLANT

Number of motors 1   Rated 1520 horsepower each at 15,000 ft. altitude.

Description: DB 605A, 12 cyl., liquid cooled, inverted "V".

Propellers: 3-blade, metal, Piaggio, variable pitch.

Superchargers: _____

Misc.: Engine built by Fiat under license. Exhaust stubs covered top and bottom by flat strips with short intake at front to direct cold air flow.

ARMAMENT

(F - fixed. M - free.)

For'd fuselage: 2 x 12.7 mm (F) 350 r.p.g.
For'd wings: 2 x 7.7 mm (F)
Through hub: _____
Dorsal: _____
Lateral: _____
Ventral: _____
Tail: _____

BOMB/FREIGHT LOAD

Normal bomb load: _____ lbs.
Max. bomb load: _____ lbs.
Typical bomb stowage: _____
_____ lbs.
Alternate bomb stowage: _____
_____ lbs.
Freight and/or troops: _____ lbs.

ARMOR

Frontal: _____
Windshield: 2" b.p. glass
Pilot's seat: Back, 8 mm.
             Head, 8 mm.
Dorsal: _____
Lateral: _____
Ventral: _____
Bulkhead: _____
Engine: _____

SPECIFICATIONS

Materials: All metal, stressed skin.

Span: 34'-8"   Length: 29'-1"   Height: 11'-6"   Wing Area: (gross) 181 sq. ft.

Weights: landing _____ lbs.; normal load 7,200 lbs.; max. load _____ lbs.

Misc.: _____

ADDITIONAL TECHNICAL DATA

ITALY	Re 2000	JULY
106		1943

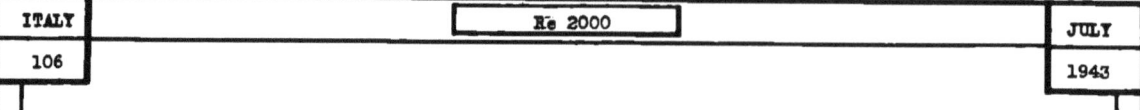

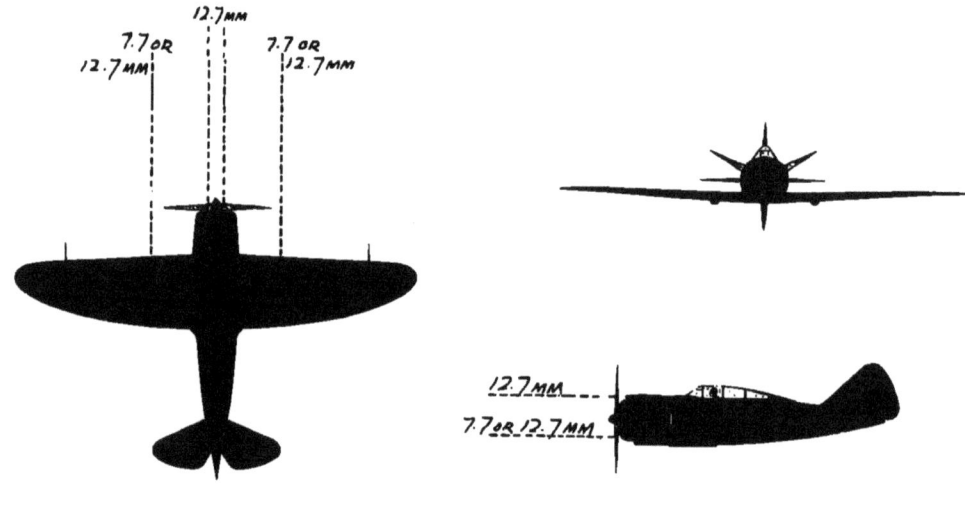

Re 2000

DESCRIPTION

The Re 2000 is an obsolescent fighter that was designed after the Seversky model as embodied in the U.S. P-35. It has been replaced by the newer Re 2001.

This aircraft is a single-engine, low-wing monoplane. Leading edges of wing are straight-tapered, trailing edges curved, tips nearly pointed. The cockpit is long and transparent. Fin and rudder are of long chord. Landing gear retracts rearward into wings, with fairings appearing as slight bulges beneath the wings.

JULY 1943 — Re 2000 — ITALY — 106

SINGLE SEAT FIGHTER "FALCO I" (FALCON)

Mfr.: OFFICINO MECCANICHE "REGGIANE" S.A.   Crew: ONE

Duty: FIGHTING, GROUND ATTACK, POSSIBLY BOMBING.

PERFORMANCE

Max. speed **325** m.p.h. at **15,000** ft. altitude; 280 mph at sea level.

Cruising speed: normal **272** m.p.h.; economical **173** m.p.h.; at **15,000** ft. altitude.

Climb: to **15,000** ft. altitude in **6.8** min. (normal load); in 10 min. (with max. load)

Fuel: normal **95** U.S. gals.; max. **383** U.S. gals. For ½ hr. combat: 49 gals.

Service ceiling: normal load **32,000** ft.; max. bomb/fuel load **26,000** ft.; min. fuel/no bombs _____ ft.

RANGES

Speeds	With Normal Fuel/Bomb Load	With Max. Bomb Load	With Max. Fuel Load
Normal cruising	400 miles	miles	1865 miles
Economical cruising	535 miles	miles	2175 miles

POWER PLANT

Number of motors **1**   Rated **1000** horsepower each at **13,000** ft. altitude.

Description: Piaggio P.XI R.C.40, 14 cyl., twin-row, air-cooled radial.

Propellers: 3-blade, metal, variable pitch.

Superchargers:

Misc.: Long chord cowling with controllable gills. Air intake above cowling.

ARMAMENT

(F - fixed. M - free.)

For'd fuselage: 2 x 12.7 mm (F)

For'd wings: Provision for 2 x 7.7/12.7 mm.

Through hub:
Dorsal:
Lateral:
Ventral:
Tail:

BOMB/FREIGHT LOAD

Normal bomb load: _____ lbs.
Max. bomb load: _____ lbs.
Typical bomb stowage:

_____ lbs.
Alternate bomb stowage:

_____ lbs.
Freight and/or troops:
_____ lbs.

ARMOR

Frontal:
Windshield:
Pilot's seat:

Dorsal:
Lateral:
Ventral:
Bulkhead:

Engine:

SPECIFICATIONS

Materials: Metal, stressed skin.

Span: **36'-1"**   Length: **25'-9"**   Height: **12'**   Wing Area: (gross) 220 sq.ft.

Weights: landing **5,200** lbs.; normal load **5,800** lbs.; max. load **7,700** lbs.

Misc.: Nardi bomb carriers (pneumatic or mechanical) suited for dive release, can be fitted in wings.

ADDITIONAL TECHNICAL DATA

With 171 U.S. gals. range is 785 miles at normal cruising, 1,040 miles at economical cruising. Manufacturer is a Caproni concern.

| ITALY 107 | Re 2001 | JULY 1943 |

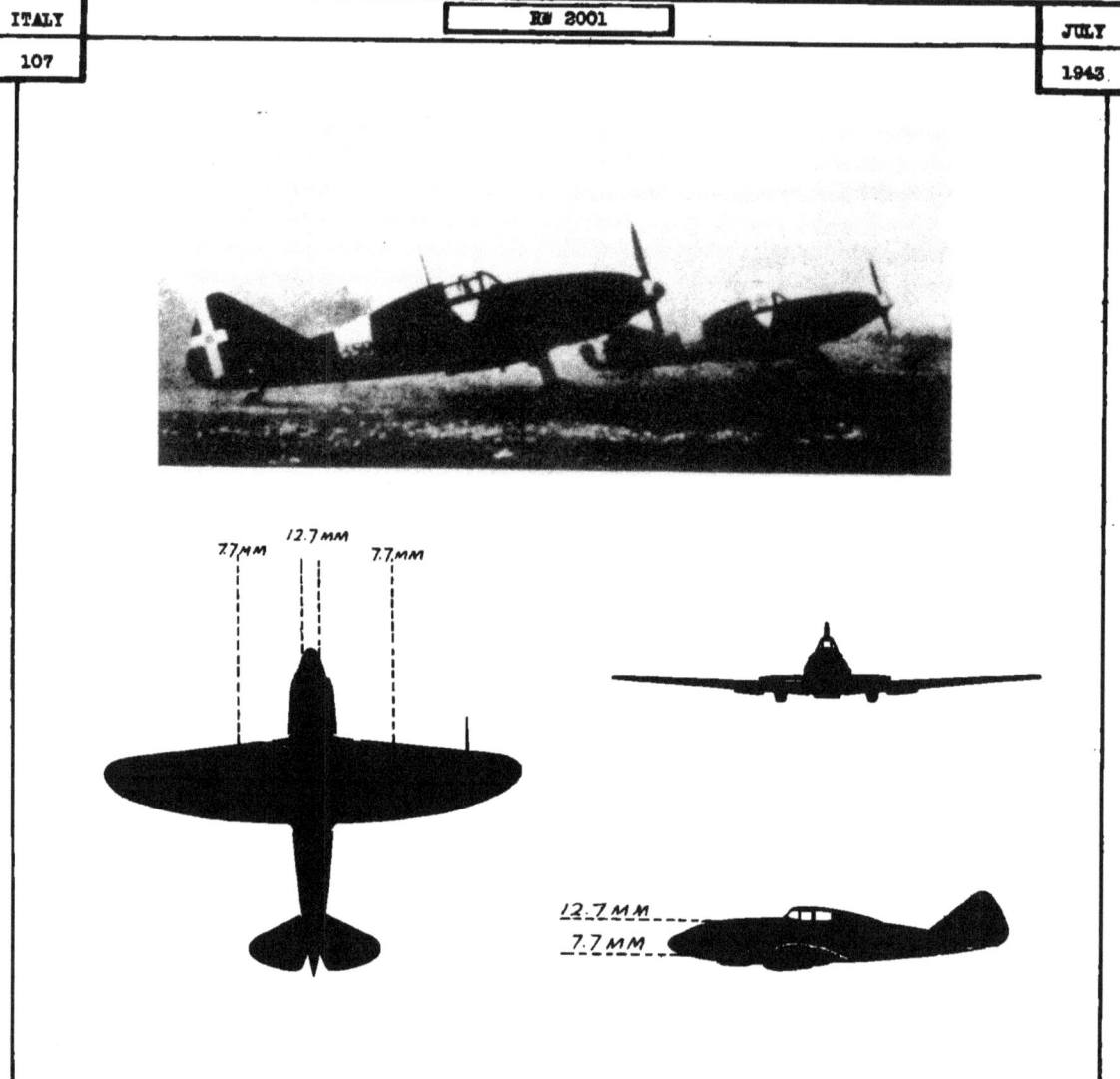

Re 2001

DESCRIPTION

The Re 2001 is one of the leading fighters of the I.A.F., although inferior to the MC 202 and 205. It is likely to be encountered wherever Italian fighters are operating.

This aircraft is a single-engine, low-wing monoplane. Wings' leading edges are straight-tapered, trailing edges are curved, tips nearly pointed. Cockpit has head fairing that merges aft into fuselage. The fin and rudder are of long chord. The landing gear retracts rearward with fairings appearing as slight bulges beneath the wings. Tailwheel is non-retractable.

RE 2005

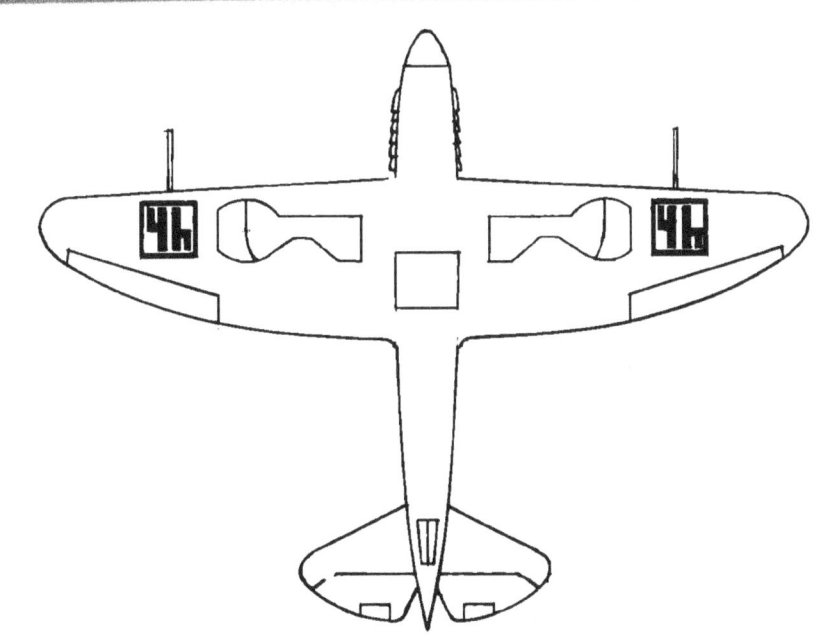

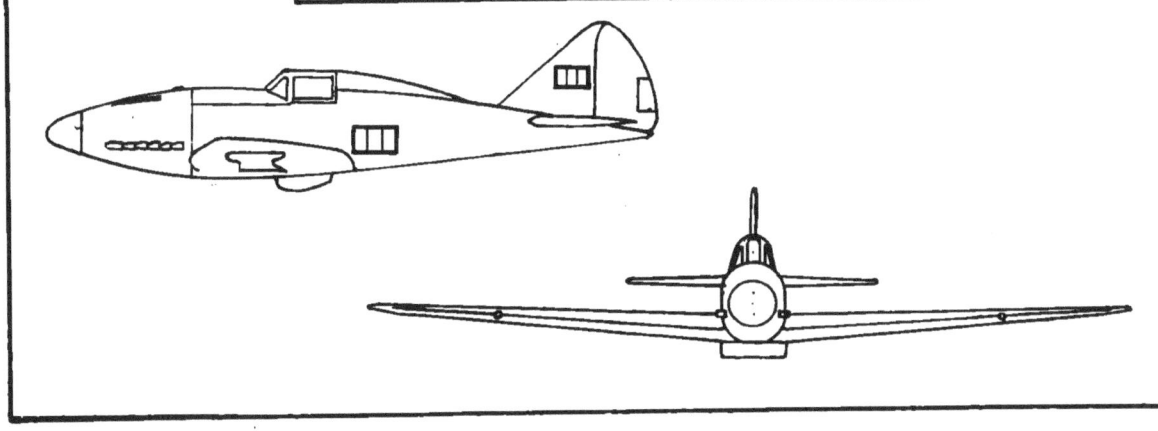

JULY 1943 — ITALY — 107

Re 2001

SINGLE-ENGINE FIGHTER "FALCO II" (FALCON)

Mfr.: OFFICINE MECCANICHE "REGGIANE" S.A.   Crew: ONE

Duty: FIGHTING. GROUND ATTACK. POSSIBLY BOMBING.

PERFORMANCE

Max. speed **350** m.p.h. at **20,000** ft. altitude; 290 mph at sea level.

Cruising speed: normal **300** m.p.h.; economical **195** m.p.h.; at **18,000** ft. altitude.

Climb: to **18,000** ft. altitude in **8.3** min.

Fuel: normal **176** U.S. gals.; max. _____ U.S. gals. For ½ hr. combat: 47 gals.

Service ceiling: normal load **34,000** ft.; max. bomb/fuel load _____ ft.; min. fuel/no bombs **36,000** ft.

RANGES

Speeds	With Normal Fuel/Bomb Load	With Max. Bomb Load	With Max. Fuel Load
Normal cruising	730 miles	_____ miles	_____ miles
Economical cruising	940 miles	_____ miles	_____ miles

POWER PLANT

Number of motors **1**   Rated **1,150** horsepower each at **16,000** ft. altitude.

Description: DB 601 A/A/1, 12 cyl., liquid-cooled, inverted "V".

Propellers: 3-blade, metal, constant speed, Fiat-Hamilton type.

Superchargers: Long intake embodying air cleaner.

Misc.: Oil radiator under engine. Coolant radiators, one under each wing, as on the Me 109. Rearward-facing exhaust stubs.

ARMAMENT

(F - fixed. M - free.)

For'd fuselage: 2 x 12.7 mm (F) 300 r.p.g.
For'd wings: 2 x 7.7 mm (F) 600 r.p.g.
Through hub: _____
Dorsal: _____
Lateral: _____
Ventral: _____
Tail: _____

BOMB/FREIGHT LOAD

Normal bomb load: _____ lbs.
Max. bomb load: **550** lbs.
Typical bomb stowage: Under fuselage.
    1 x 550 lbs.
Alternate bomb stowage: _____

Freight and/or troops: _____ lbs. / _____ lbs.

ARMOR

Frontal: _____
Windshield: _____
Pilot's seat: Bottom, 7 mm. Head & shoulder, 9 mm.
Dorsal: _____
Lateral: _____
Ventral: _____
Bulkhead: _____
Engine: _____

SPECIFICATIONS

Materials: Metal, stressed skin.

Span: **36'**   Length: **27'-4"**   Height: **12'**   Wing Area: (gross) **220** sq. ft.

Weights: landing **5,800** lbs.; normal load **7,000** lbs.; max. load _____ lbs.

Misc.: _____

ADDITIONAL TECHNICAL DATA

Sub-type IIA identified. Nardi bomb carriers (pneumatic or mechanical) suitable for dive release can be fitted in wings.

SAI 207

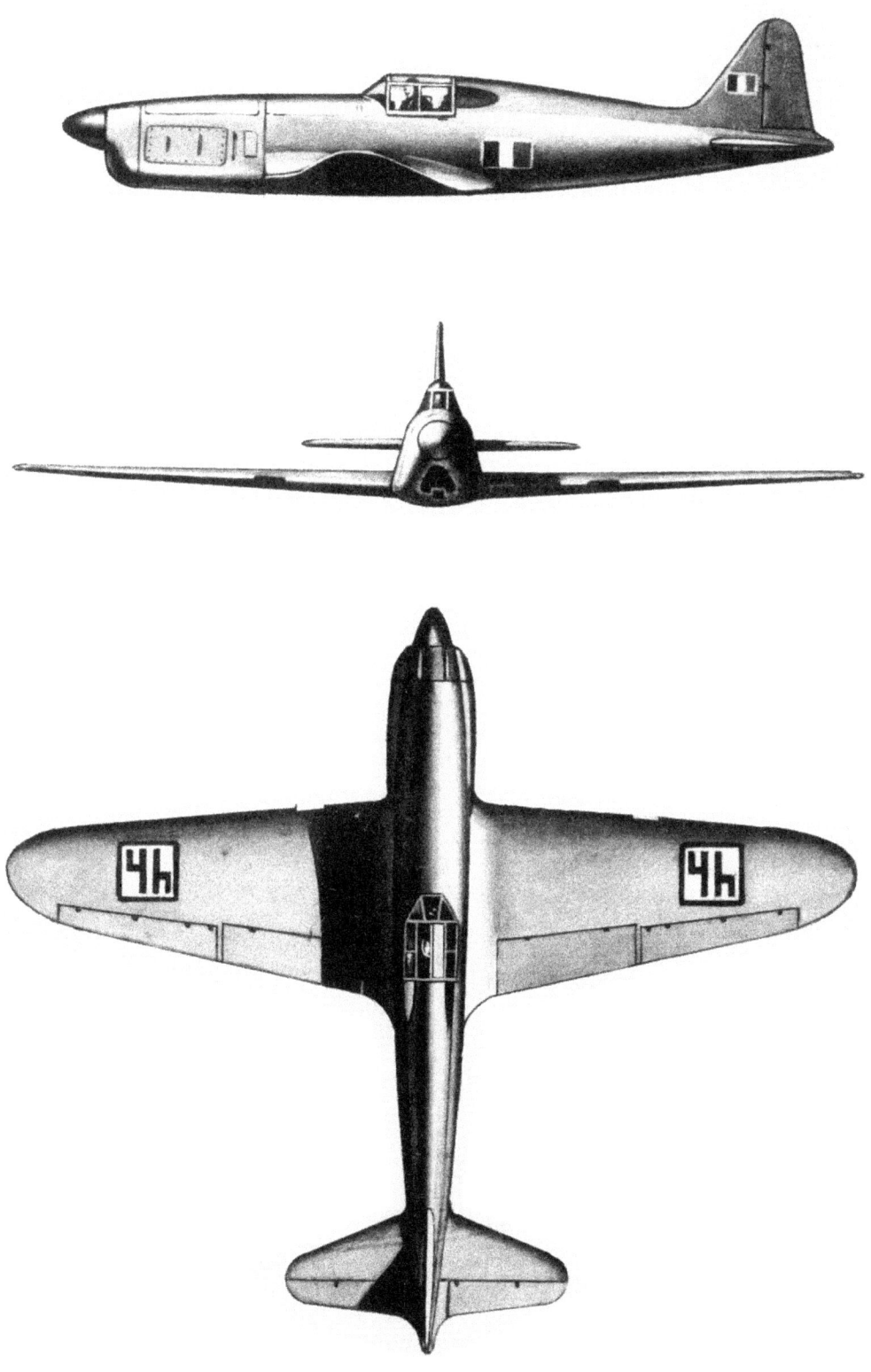

Mfr.: _____ Crew: _____
Duty: _____

PERFORMANCE

Max. speed _____ m.p.h. at _____ ft. altitude.

Cruising speed: normal _____ m.p.h.; economical _____ m.p.h.; at _____ ft. altitude.

Climb: to _____ ft. altitude in _____ min. _____

Fuel: normal _____ U.S. gals.; max. _____ U.S. gals. _____

Service ceiling: normal load _____ ft.; max. bomb/fuel load _____ ft.; min. fuel/no bombs _____ ft.

RANGES

Speeds	With Normal Fuel/Bomb Load	With Max. Bomb Load	With Max. Fuel Load
Normal cruising	_____ miles	_____ miles	_____ miles
Economical cruising	_____ miles	_____ miles	_____ miles

POWER PLANT

Number of motors _____ Rated _____ horsepower each at _____ ft. altitude.

Description: _____

Propellers: _____

Superchargers: _____

Misc.: _____

ARMAMENT

(F - fixed. M - free.)

For'd fuselage: _____
For'd wings: _____
Through hub: _____
Dorsal: _____
Lateral: _____
Ventral: _____
Tail: _____

BOMB/FREIGHT LOAD

Normal bomb load: _____ lbs.
Max. bomb load: _____ lbs.
Typical bomb stowage: _____
_____ lbs.
Alternate bomb stowage:
_____ lbs.
Freight and/or troops: _____ lbs.

ARMOR

Frontal: _____
Windshield: _____
Pilot's seat: _____
Dorsal: _____
Lateral: _____
Ventral: _____
Bulkhead: _____
Engine: _____

SPECIFICATIONS

Materials: _____

Span: _____ Length: _____ Height: _____ Wing Area: _____

Weights: landing _____ lbs.; normal load _____ lbs.; max. load _____ lbs.

Misc.: _____

ADDITIONAL TECHNICAL DATA

_____
_____
_____
_____

ITALY	Ba 88	JULY
201		1943

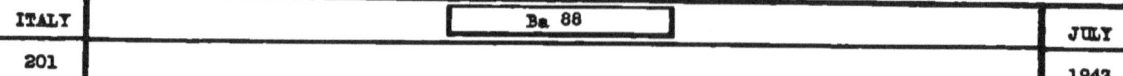

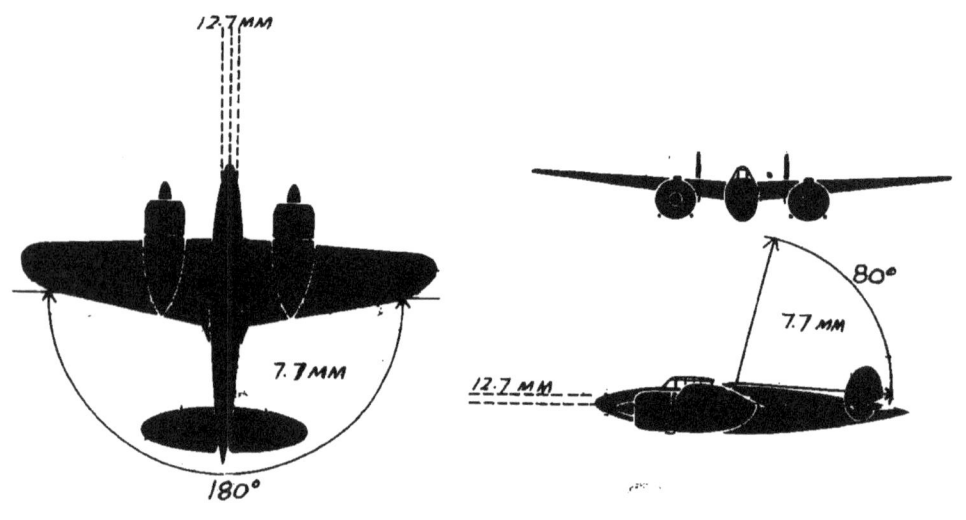

Ba 88

DESCRIPTION

The Ba 88 is an obsolescent aircraft originally designed as a fighter but subsequently employed for light bombing, ground attack and reconnaissance operations. It probably is in service in small numbers.

This aircraft is a twin-engine, shoulder-wing monoplane. Wings taper, more so on trailing than leading edges; tips are rounded. Handley-Page leading edge slots, slotted ailerons and slotted flaps are fitted. Fuselage is of oval section. The twin fins and rudders are set in from tips of the stabilizer which is braced. Landing gear retracts rearward into engine nacelles; tail wheel retracts.

JULY 1943 — Ba 88 — ITALY 201

TWIN-ENGINE BOMBER "LINCE" (LYNX)

Mfr.: BREDA Crew: TWO
Duty: LIGHT BOMBING. GROUND ATTACK. RECONNAISSANCE.

PERFORMANCE

Max. speed 300 m.p.h. at 15,000 ft. altitude; 256 mph at sea level.
Cruising speed: normal 255 m.p.h.; economical 185 m.p.h.; at 15,000 ft. altitude.
Climb: to 15,000 ft. altitude in 10 min. (normal load); in 11.2 min. (with max. load).
Fuel: normal (est.) 422 U.S. gals.; max. (est.) 518 U.S. gals. For ½ hr. combat: 96 gals.
Service ceiling: normal load 27,000 ft.; max. bomb/fuel load 26,000 ft.; min. fuel/no bombs 31,000 ft.

RANGES

Speeds	With Normal Fuel/Bomb Load	With Max. Bomb Load	With Max. Fuel Load
Normal cruising	935 miles	930 miles	1,160 miles
Economical cruising	1,100 miles	1,100 miles	1,370 miles

POWER PLANT

Number of motors 2 Rated 1,000 horsepower each at 13,150 ft. altitude.
Description: Piaggio P.XI RC.40, 14 cyl., twin-row, air-cooled radial.
Propellers: 3-blade, V.D.M. or Piaggio.
Superchargers:
Misc.: Long chord cowlings with controllable gills. Air intakes above cowlings.

ARMAMENT
(F - fixed. M - free.)
For'd fuselage: 3 x 12.7mm (F)
For'd wings:
Through hub:
Dorsal: 1 x 7.7mm (M)
Lateral:
Ventral:
Tail:

BOMB/FREIGHT LOAD
Normal bomb load: _____ lbs.
Max. bomb load: 660 lbs.
Typical bomb stowage:
    3 x 220 lbs.
Alternate bomb stowage:
    _____ lbs.
Freight and/or troops: _____ lbs.

ARMOR
Frontal:
Windshield:
Pilot's seat:
Dorsal:
Lateral:
Ventral:
Bulkhead:
Engine:

SPECIFICATIONS

Materials: Welded steel tube and duralumin; metal skin covering.
Span: 50'-10" Length: 37'-10" Height: _____ Wing Area: (gross) 358 sq.ft.
Weights: landing 12,000 lbs.; normal load 14,700 lbs.; max. load 15,400 lbs.
Misc.: Wing and fuselage of welded steel tubing.

ADDITIONAL TECHNICAL DATA

Nose guns are offset to port. Rear gun is not in a turret but on a track type mounting, possibly power-assisted.

ITALY	BR 20M	JULY
202		1943

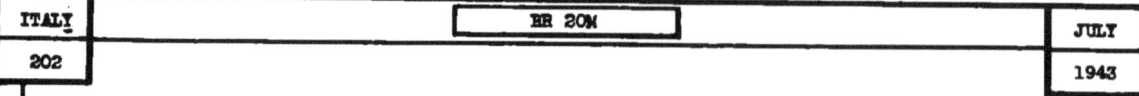

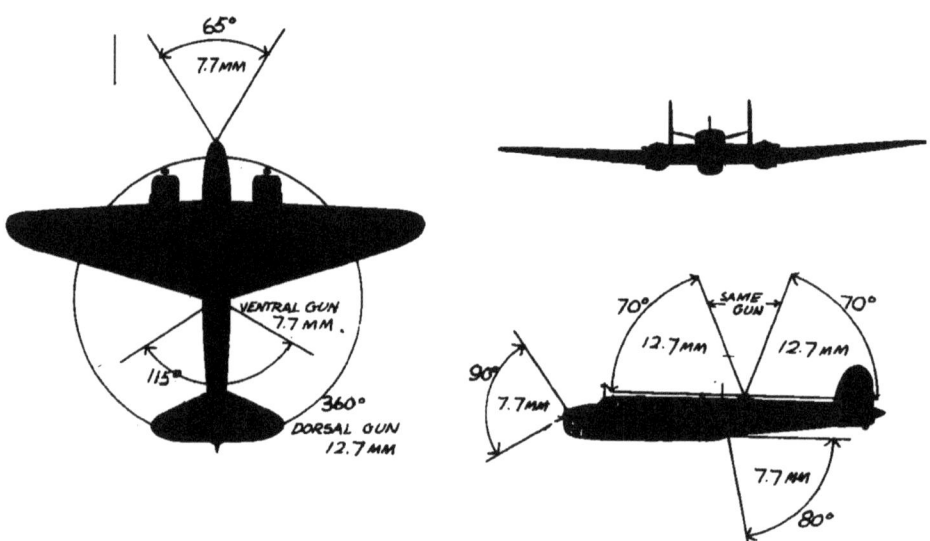

BR 20M

DESCRIPTION

The BR 20M is an obsolescent bomber, probably used more for reconnaissance than bombing. "BR" denotes "Bombardamento Rosatelli", or bomber designed by Rosatelli

The aircraft is a twin-engine, mid-wing monoplane. Wings taper to rounded tips. Split flaps are fitted. Fuselage is of rectangular section with rounded corners. There are twin braced fins and rudders set inboard of stabilizer tips. Landing gear retracts rearward into nacelles.

| JULY 1943 | BR 20M | ITALY 202 |

TWIN-ENGINE BOMBER "CICOGNA" (STORK)

Mfr.: **FIAT** Crew: **FOUR**
Duty: **BOMBING. RECONNAISSANCE.**

PERFORMANCE

Max. speed **255** m.p.h. at **13,500** ft. altitude.
Cruising speed: normal **217** m.p.h.; economical **175** m.p.h.; at **13,000** ft. altitude.
Climb: to **13,000** ft. altitude in **14** min. (normal load); in 19 min. (with max. load).
Fuel: normal **639** U.S. gals.; max. **962** U.S. gals.
Service ceiling: normal load **25,000** ft.; max. bomb/fuel load **31,500** ft.; min. fuel/no bombs **23,000** ft.

RANGES

Speeds	With Normal Fuel/Bomb Load	With Max. Bomb Load (with 771 gals.)	With Max. Fuel Load (+ 2,200 lbs. bombs)
Normal cruising	1,210 miles	1,450 miles	1,835 miles
Economical cruising	1,350 miles	1,500 miles	1,890 miles

POWER PLANT

Number of motors **2** Rated **1,000** horsepower each at **13,500** ft. altitude.
Description: **Fiat A.80 RC.41, 14 cyl., twin-row, air-cooled radial.**
Propellers: **3-blade, Fiat-Hamilton, constant speed.**
Superchargers:
Misc.: **Long chord cowlings.**

ARMAMENT
(F - fixed. M - free.)
For'd fuselage: 1 x 7.7mm (M)
For'd wings:
Through hub:
Dorsal: 1 x 12.7mm (M)
Lateral:
Ventral: 1 x 7.7mm (M)
Tail:

BOMB/FREIGHT LOAD
Normal bomb load: **2,200** lbs.
Max. bomb load: **3,500** lbs.
Typical bomb stowage:
 4 x 550 lbs.
Alternate bomb stowage:
 2 x 1100 lbs.
 2 x 1760 lbs.
Freight and/or troops: _____ lbs.

ARMOR
Frontal:
Windshield:
Pilot's seat: **Protected back and below.**
Dorsal: **Upper part of gunner's body protected.**
Ventral:
Bulkhead:
Engine:

SPECIFICATIONS

Materials: **Steel tubing, fabric and metal covering.**
Span: **70'-6"** Length: **52'-10"** Height: **14'-1"** Wing Area: (gross) **796** sq.ft.
Weights: landing **16,300** lbs.; normal load **22,500** lbs.; max. load _____ lbs.
Misc.: **Wing of duralumin spars and built-up tubular ribs. Fuselage of welded steel tubing, with light metal secondary structure.**

ADDITIONAL TECHNICAL DATA

Nose turret is manually-operated. Top turret is semi-retractable and power-operated.
Ventral gun mounting manually-operated and semi-retractable.
Nov 1940 used in ___ ___, escorted by CR42s

ITALY	Ca 135 bis	JULY
203		1943

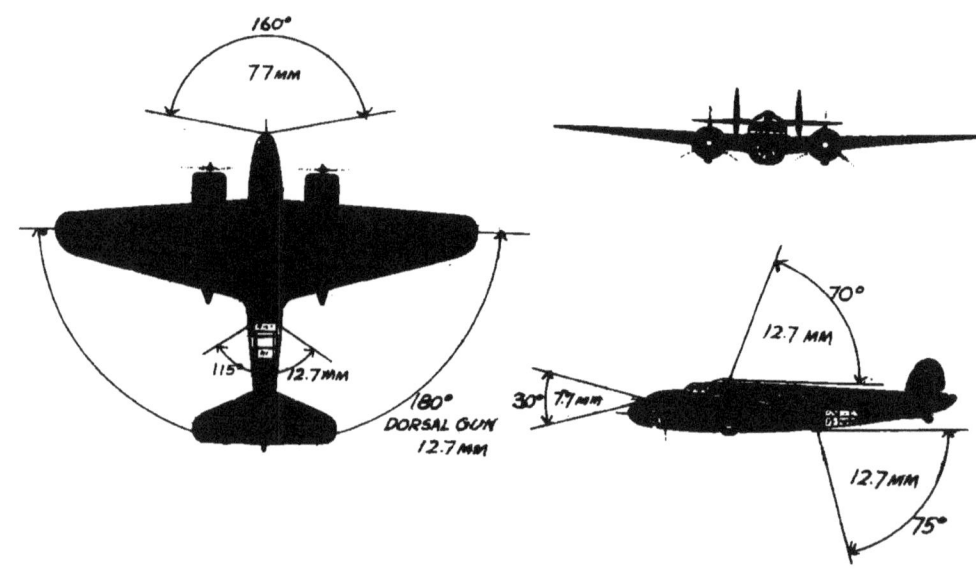

Ca 135 bis

DESCRIPTION

The Ca 135 bis is an obsolescent reconnaissance bomber that probably still remains in service. It is a twin-engine, mid-wing monoplane. Wing has deep chord and moderate taper to rounded tips. Outer wing panels have detachable tips, trailing and leading edges. Split flaps are fitted between ailerons and fuselage. The forward fuselage has a large amount of transparent panelling. Twin fins and rudders are set in from stabilizer tips. Landing gear retracts rearward into engine nacelles.

JULY 1943 — ITALY — 203

Ca 135 bis

TWIN-ENGINE BOMBER

Mfr.: **CAPRONI** Crew: **FOUR to FIVE**
Duty: **BOMBING, RECONNAISSANCE**

PERFORMANCE

Max. speed **270** m.p.h. at **15,000** ft. altitude; 235 mph at sea level.
Cruising speed: normal **230** m.p.h.; economical **185** m.p.h.; at **15,000** ft. altitude.
Climb: to **15,000** ft. altitude in **15** min.
Fuel: normal **566** U.S. gals.; max. **729** U.S. gals.
Service ceiling: normal load **24,500** ft.; max. bomb/fuel load _____ ft.; min. fuel/no bombs **31,000** ft.

RANGES

Speeds	With Normal Fuel/Bomb Load	With Max. Bomb Load	With Max. Fuel Load (and 1,100 lbs. bombs)
Normal cruising	1,125 miles	1,000 miles	1,475 miles
Economical cruising	1,250 miles	1,100 miles	1,650 miles

POWER PLANT

Number of motors **2** Rated **1,000** horsepower each at **13,100** ft. altitude.
Description: **Piaggio P.XI RC.40, 14 cyl., twin-row air-cooled radial.**
Propellers: **3-blade, Fiat-Hamilton, constant speed.**
Superchargers: _____
Misc.: **Long chord cowlings with controllable gills.**

ARMAMENT

(F - fixed. M - free.)
For'd fuselage: 1 x 7.7mm (M)
For'd wings:
Through hub:
Dorsal: 1 x 12.7mm (M)
Lateral:
Ventral: 1 x 12.7mm (M)
Tail:

BOMB/FREIGHT LOAD

Normal bomb load: 2,200 lbs.
Max. bomb load: 2,640 lbs.
Typical bomb stowage: Internal
_____ lbs.
Alternate bomb stowage:
_____ lbs.
Freight and/or troops: _____ lbs.

ARMOR

Frontal:
Windshield:
Pilot's seat:
Dorsal:
Lateral:
Ventral:
Bulkhead:
Engine:

SPECIFICATIONS

Materials: **Welded steel tube, wood, fabric, plywood.**
Span: **61'-8"** Length: **44'-11"** Height: **11'-1"** Wing Area: (gross) **645 sq.ft.**
Weights: landing **15,200** lbs.; normal load **20,800** lbs.; max. load _____ lbs.
Misc.: **Wings of wooden box spars, plywood and fabric covering. Fuselage of welded steel tube, metal, plywood and fabric covering.**

ADDITIONAL TECHNICAL DATA

Dorsal gun is in manually-operated turret; nose gun transverse slot; ventral gun on retractable mounting.

ITALY 204 | Ca 310 | JULY 1943

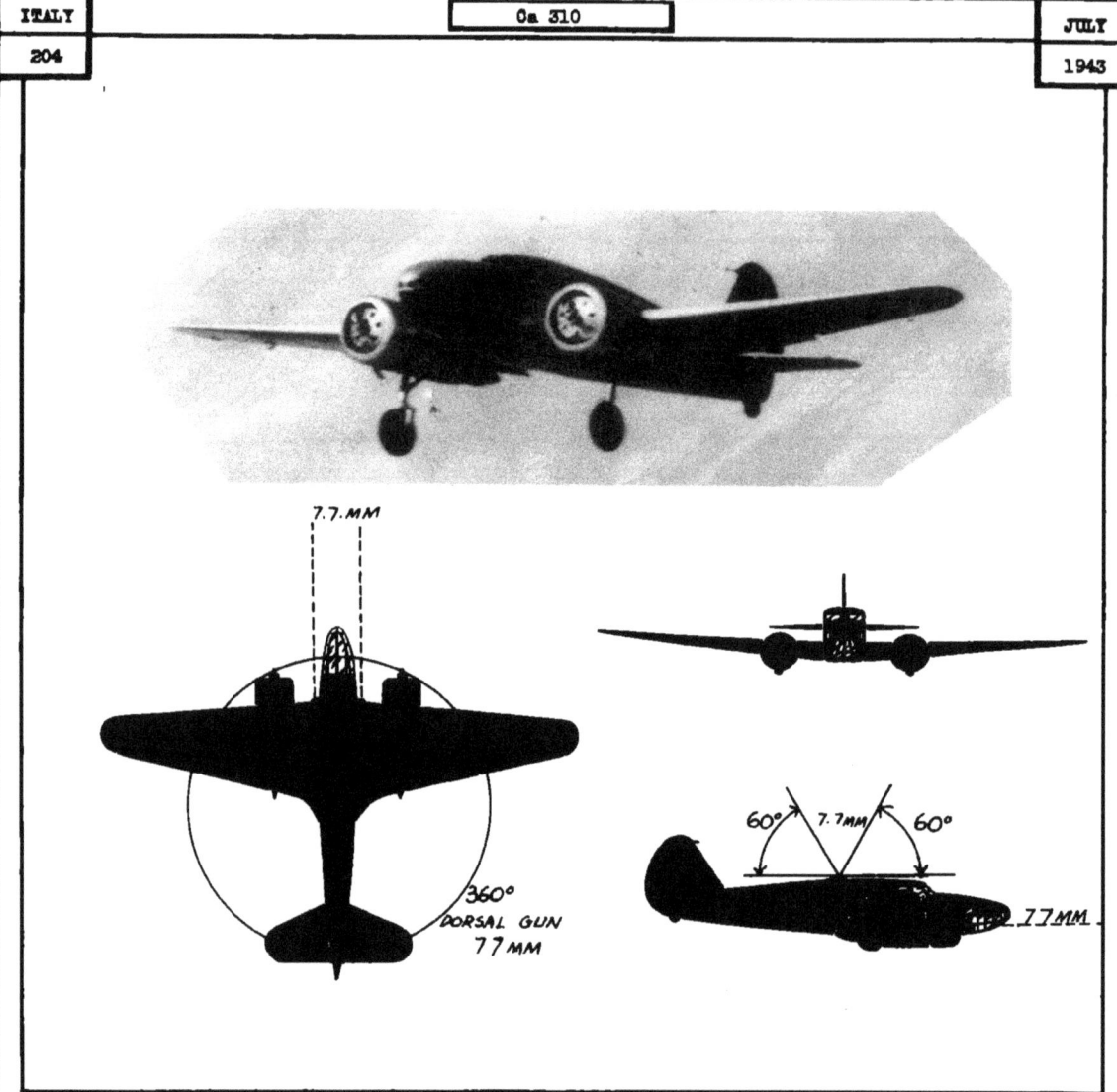

Ca 310

DESCRIPTION

The Ca 310 reconnaissance bomber appears to be in service in small numbers.

The aircraft is a twin-engine, low-wing monoplane. Wings taper to rounded tips. Split flaps are fitted. Cockpit is over the leading edge. The bottom of the nose is made of transparent panelling. There is a single fin and rudder. Landing gear retracts rearward into nacelles.

JULY 1943 — ITALY — 204

Ca 310

THREE-ENGINE BOMBER "LIBECCIO" (SIROCCO)

Mfr.: **CAPRONI** Crew: **THREE**
Duty: **BOMBING, RECONNAISSANCE**

PERFORMANCE

Max. speed **230** m.p.h. at **13,000** ft. altitude; 212 mph at sea level.

Cruising speed: normal **200** m.p.h.; economical **150** m.p.h.; at **13,000** ft. altitude.

Climb: to **13,000** ft. altitude in **12** min.

Fuel: normal (est.) **300** U.S. gals.; max. _____ U.S. gals.

Service ceiling: normal load **25,000** ft.; max. bomb/fuel load _____ ft.; min. fuel/no bombs **29,000** ft.

RANGES

Speeds	With Normal Fuel/Bomb Load	With Max. Bomb Load	With Max. Fuel Load
Normal cruising	1,125 miles	600 miles	_____ miles
Economical cruising	1,300 miles	700 miles	_____ miles

POWER PLANT

Number of motors **2** Rated **460** horsepower each at **11,500** ft. altitude.

Description: **Piaggio P.VII c.35, 7 cyl., air-cooled radial.**

Propellers: **2-blade, variable pitch.**

Superchargers: _____

Misc.: **Top sections of medium chord cowlings carried back over nacelles.**

ARMAMENT

(F - fixed. M - free.)

For'd fuselage: _____
For'd wings: **1/2 x 7.7mm (F)**
Through hub: _____
Dorsal: **1 x 7.7 mm (M)**
Lateral: _____
Ventral: _____
Tail: _____

BOMB/FREIGHT LOAD

Normal bomb load: **880** lbs.
Max. bomb load: _____ lbs.
Typical bomb stowage: _____

    4 x 220 lbs.
Alternate bomb stowage:

    2 x 440 lbs.
Freight and/or troops: _____ lbs.

ARMOR

Frontal: _____
Windshield: _____
Pilot's seat: _____
Dorsal: _____
Lateral: _____
Ventral: _____
Bulkhead: _____
Engine: _____

SPECIFICATIONS

Materials: **Metal, wood, fabric.**

Span: **53'-1"** Length: **40'** Height: **11'-6"** Wing Area (gross) **418** sq.ft.

Weights: landing **8,400** lbs.; normal load **10,250** lbs.; max. load _____ lbs.

Misc.: **Wing of two box spars, plywood and fabric covering. Fuselage of welded steel tubing, metal and fabric covered.**

ADDITIONAL TECHNICAL DATA

Dorsal gun in manually-operated turret, probably with indirect sighting.

ITALY	Ca 311, 312 bis	JULY
205		1943

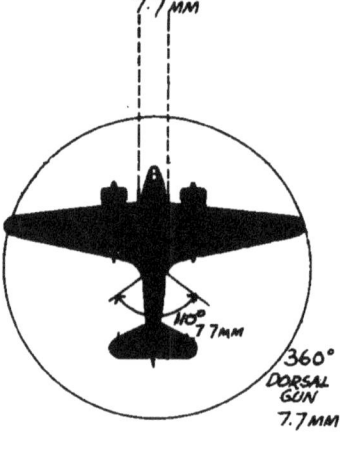

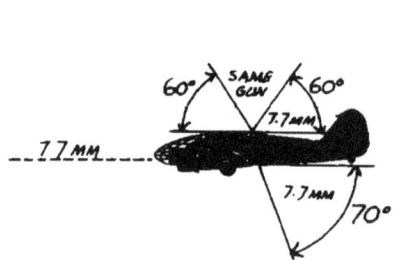

Ca 311, 312 bis

DESCRIPTION

The Ca 311 and 312 bis landplanes are essentially similar aircraft, a number of which appear to be operational.

They are twin-engine, low-wing monoplanes. Wings taper moderately to rounded tips. Blunt nose is almost completely transparent. There is a large amount of transparent panelling in the sides of the fuselage. Landing gear retracts rearward into engine nacelles.

JULY 1943 — ITALY 205

Ca 311, 312 bis

SIMILAR TWIN-ENGINE BOMBERS (LANDPLANES).

Mfr.: **CAPRONI.** Crew: **THREE to FOUR.**
Duty: **BOMBING. RECONNAISSANCE. POSSIBLY TORPEDO-DROPPING.**

PERFORMANCE

Max. speed **260** m.p.h. at **13,000** ft. altitude; 235 mph at sea level.

Cruising speed: normal **222** m.p.h.; economical **160** m.p.h.; at **13,000** ft. altitude.

Climb: to **13,000** ft. altitude in **9.3** min.

Fuel: normal **286** U.S. gals.; max. **420** U.S. gals.

Service ceiling: normal load **27,000** ft.; max. bomb/fuel load _____ ft.; min. fuel/no bombs **32,000** ft.

RANGES

Speeds	With Normal Fuel/Bomb Load	With Max. Bomb Load	With Max. Fuel Load
Normal cruising	870 miles	miles	1,285 miles
Economical cruising	1,070 miles	miles	1,585 miles

POWER PLANT

Number of motors **2** Rated **640** horsepower each at **11,500** ft. altitude.

Description: **Piaggio P.XVI RC.35, 9 cyl., air-cooled radial.**

Propellers: **3-blade, metal. (older versions: 2-blade).**

Superchargers:

Misc.: **Long chord cowling.**

ARMAMENT
(F - fixed. M - free.)
For'd fuselage:
For'd wings: **1/2 x 7.7 mm (F)**
Through hub:
Dorsal: **1 x 7.7 mm (M)**
Lateral:
Ventral: **Possibly 1x7.7mm(M)**
Tail:

BOMB/FREIGHT LOAD
Normal bomb load: **880** lbs.
Max. bomb load: _____ lbs.
Typical bomb stowage:
  4 x 220 lbs.
Alternate bomb stowage:
  8 x 110 lbs.
Freight and/or troops: _____ lbs.

ARMOR
Frontal:
Windshield:
Pilot's seat:
Dorsal:
Lateral:
Ventral:
Bulkhead:
Engine:

SPECIFICATIONS

Materials: **Metal, wood, fabric.**

Span: **53'-4"** Length: **38'-5"** Height: **10'-6"** Wing Area (gross) **417** sq.ft.

Weights: landing **9,400** lbs.; normal load **12,000** lbs.; max. load _____ lbs.

Misc.: **Wooden wings of two box spars and plywood covering. Fuselage of welded steel tube framework, fabric covering over light subsidiary structure.**

ADDITIONAL TECHNICAL DATA

Dorsal gun in shallow, manually-operated turret.

ITALY 206 | Ca 313 | JULY 1943

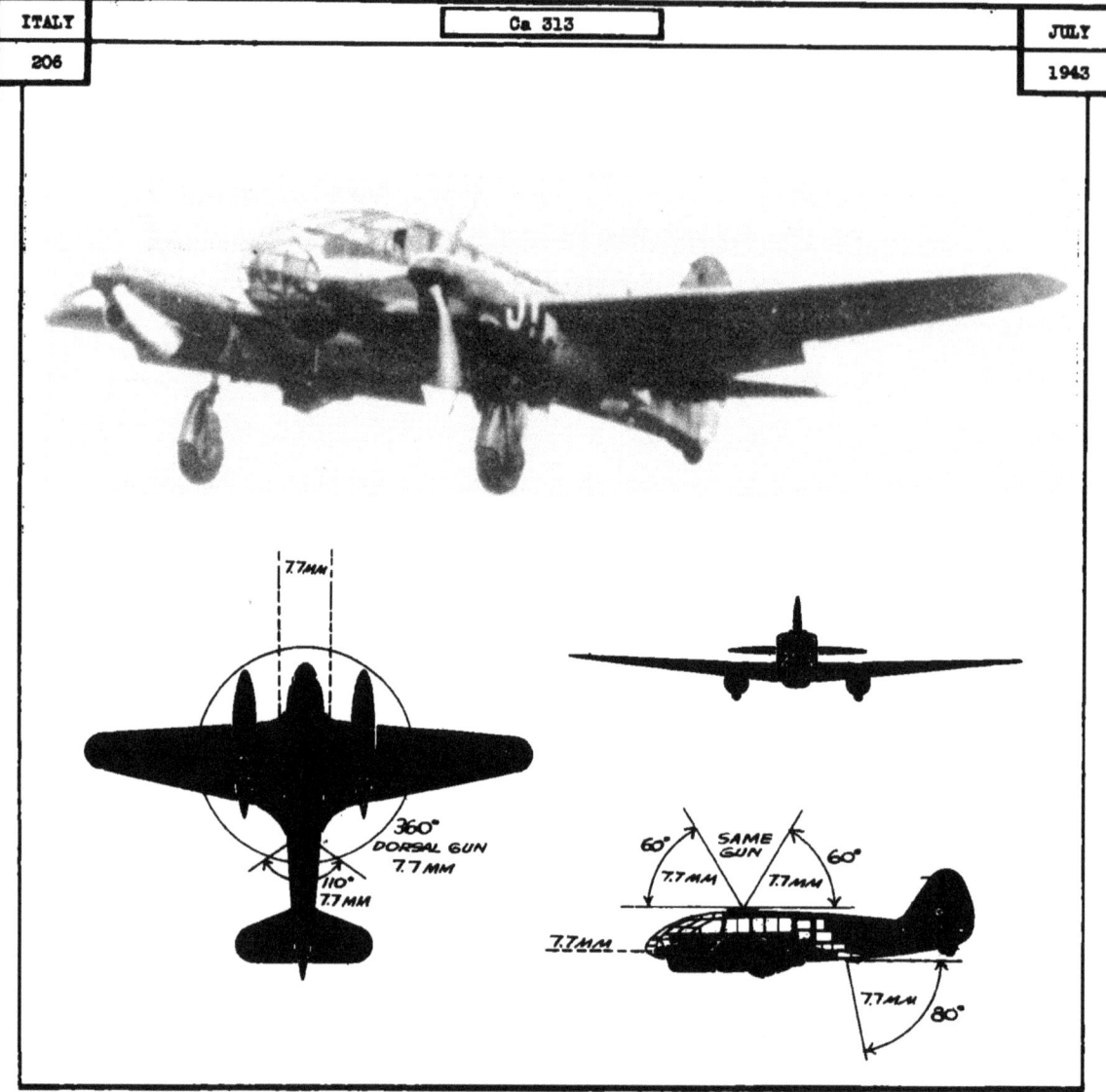

Ca 313

DESCRIPTION

The Ca 313 is a development of the Ca 310-312 series and probably will continue to remain in service.

This aircraft is a twin-engine, low-wing monoplane. Wings taper moderately to rounded tips. The blunt nose is almost completely transparent. There is a large amount of transparent panelling in the sides of the fuselage. Landing gear retracts into engine nacelles.

JULY 1943 — ITALY 206

Ca 313

TWIN-ENGINE BOMBER

Mfr.: **CAPRONI** Crew: **THREE to FOUR**
Duty: **BOMBING. RECONNAISSANCE. TORPEDO-DROPPING.**

PERFORMANCE

Max. speed **270** m.p.h. at **13,000** ft. altitude; 235 mph at sea level.
Cruising speed: normal **230** m.p.h.; economical **160** m.p.h.; at **13,000** ft. altitude.
Climb: to **13,000** ft. altitude in **8.7** min.
Fuel: normal **288** U.S. gals.; max. **420** U.S. gals.
Service ceiling: normal load **27,000** ft.; max. bomb/fuel load _____ ft.; min. fuel/no bombs **31,500** ft.

RANGES

Speeds	With Normal Fuel/Bomb Load	With Max. Bomb Load	With Max. Fuel Load
Normal cruising	755 miles	miles	1,120 miles
Economical cruising	960 miles	miles	1,510 miles

POWER PLANT

Number of motors **2** Rated **750** horsepower each at **11,500** ft. altitude.
Description: **Isotta Fraschini "Delta" RC.35, 12 cyl., air-cooled, inverted "V".**
Propellers: **3-blade, variable pitch.**
Superchargers:
Misc.:

ARMAMENT

(F - fixed. M - free.)
For'd fuselage:
For'd wings: **1/2 x 7.7 mm (F)**
Through hub:
Dorsal: **1 x 7.7 mm (M)**
Lateral:
Ventral: **Possibly 1 x 7.7 mm (M)**
Tail:

BOMB/FREIGHT LOAD

Normal bomb load: **880** lbs.
Max. bomb load: _____ lbs.
Typical bomb stowage:
_____ lbs.
Alternate bomb stowage:
Possibly 1 torpedo lbs.
Freight and/or troops: _____ lbs.

ARMOR

Frontal:
Windshield:
Pilot's seat:
Dorsal:
Lateral:
Ventral:
Bulkhead:
Engine:

SPECIFICATIONS

Materials: **Metal, wood, fabric, plywood.**
Span: **53'-5"** Length: **38'-6"** Height: **11'-8"** Wing Area: (gross) **418** sq.ft.
Weights: landing **9,800** lbs.; normal load **12,400** lbs.; max. load _____ lbs.
Misc.: **Wooden wings of two box spars and plywood covering. Fuselage of welded steel tubing, fabric covering over light subsidiary structure.**

ADDITIONAL TECHNICAL DATA

Dorsal gun is in manually-operated turret, with indirect sighting.

ITALY		JULY
207		1943

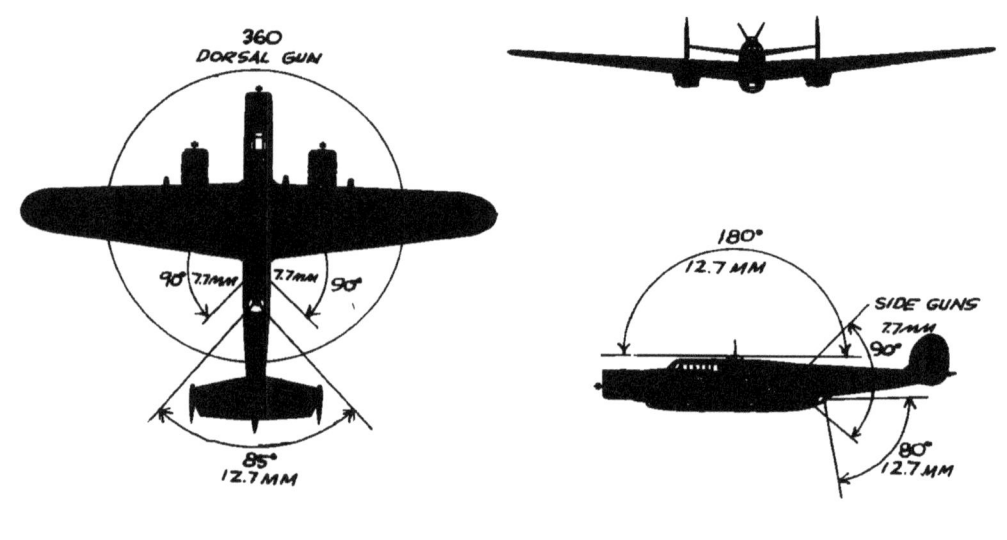

Cant Z 1007 bis

DESCRIPTION

The Cant Z 1007 bis is one of the I.A.F.'s best bombers, and it probably will remain in service in substantial numbers.

This aircraft is a three-engine, mid-wing monoplane. Wings taper moderately to rounded tips. Camber-changing flaps are fitted. Cockpit is forward of the wing. There is a break in the fuselage for the bombardier's position close behind the nose engine and the ventral gunner's position aft of the trailing edge. Later versions have twin fins and rudders, earlier models a single fin and rudder. Stabilizer is braced. Landing gear retracts rearward into nacelles.

JULY 1943 — ITALY 207

Cant Z 1007 bis

THREE-ENGINE BOMBER "ALCIONE" (KINGFISHER).

Mfr.: **CANTIERI RIUNITI.**   Crew: **FOUR to FIVE.**
Duty: **BOMBING. RECONNAISSANCE.**

PERFORMANCE

Max. speed **280** m.p.h. at **15,000** ft. altitude; 240 mph at sea level.

Cruising speed: normal **235** m.p.h.; economical **170** m.p.h.; at **15,000** ft. altitude.

Climb: to **15,000** ft. altitude in **11.7** min.

Fuel: normal (est.) **1440** U.S. gals.; max. _____ U.S. gals.

Service ceiling: normal load **26,500** ft.; max. bomb/fuel load **26,000** ft.; min. fuel/no bombs **31,500** ft.

RANGES

Speeds	With Normal Fuel/Bomb Load	With Max. Bomb Load	With Max. Fuel Load (+ 2200 lbs. bombs)
Normal cruising	920 miles	380 miles	1,530 miles
Economical cruising	1,150 miles	475 miles	1,925 miles

POWER PLANT

Number of motors **3**   Rated **1,000** horsepower each at **13,000** ft. altitude.

Description: **Piaggio P.XI RC.40, 14 cyl., twin-row, air-cooled radial.**

Propellers: **3-blade, metal, Piaggio, constant speed.**

Superchargers: _____

Misc.: **Long chord cowlings with controllable gills. 3 ft. long extension exhaust pipes in blanked off cone having 24 slots.**

ARMAMENT

(F - fixed. M - free.)

For'd fuselage: _____
For'd wings: _____
Through hub: _____
Dorsal: 1x12.7mm(M) 350 rds.
Lateral: 2x 7.7mm(M) 500 rds.
Ventral: 1x12.7mm(M)
Tail: Provision for 1 m.g.

BOMB/FREIGHT LOAD

Normal bomb load: **2,640** lbs.
Max. bomb load: **4,850** lbs.
Typical bomb stowage: Internal and external.
  20 x 220 lbs.
Alternate bomb stowage:
  20 x 44 lbs.
  3 x 1100 lbs.
Torpedo, 1 x 1848 lbs.
Freight and/or troops: _____ lbs.

ARMOR

Frontal: _____
Windshield: _____
Pilot's seat: Both pilots. 5-6 mm.
Dorsal: Gunner, 8 mm.
Lateral: 5-6 mm.
Ventral: 6 mm.
Bulkhead: 6 mm. just aft of lateral gun position.
Engine: _____

SPECIFICATIONS

Materials: **All wood, plywood and fabric covering.**

Span: **81'-10"**   Length: **61'-3"**   Height: **18'-7"**   Wing Area (gross) **810** sq.ft.

Weights: landing **21,700** lbs.; normal load **28,600** lbs.; max. load _____ lbs.

Misc.: **6 self-sealing fuel tanks in wings. Dorsal turret electro-hydraulically-operated.**

ADDITIONAL TECHNICAL DATA

Piaggio P.XIX 1,300 hp engines reported, which may increase max. speed to about 300 mph at 13,000 ft.

ITALY	CR 25	JULY
208		1943

NO SILHOUETTES AVAILABLE

CR 25

DESCRIPTION

The CR 25 is one of the lesser known reconnaissance bombers of the I.A.F. A number of these aircraft appear to be still in service. It is said to be comparable in many respects to the earlier British Blenheims. "CR" denotes "Caccia Rosatelli", fighter designed by Rosatelli.

This aircraft is a twin-engine monoplane. Wings taper to rounded tips. Split flaps are fitted. Fuselage is narrow and straight-sided. Lower part of nose has transparent panelling. Cockpit is forward of leading edge. Landing gear retracts rearward into nacelles. Tail wheel is non-retractable.

A.L. 24 to A.P. 1480 C (Section B) FIAT C.R. 25

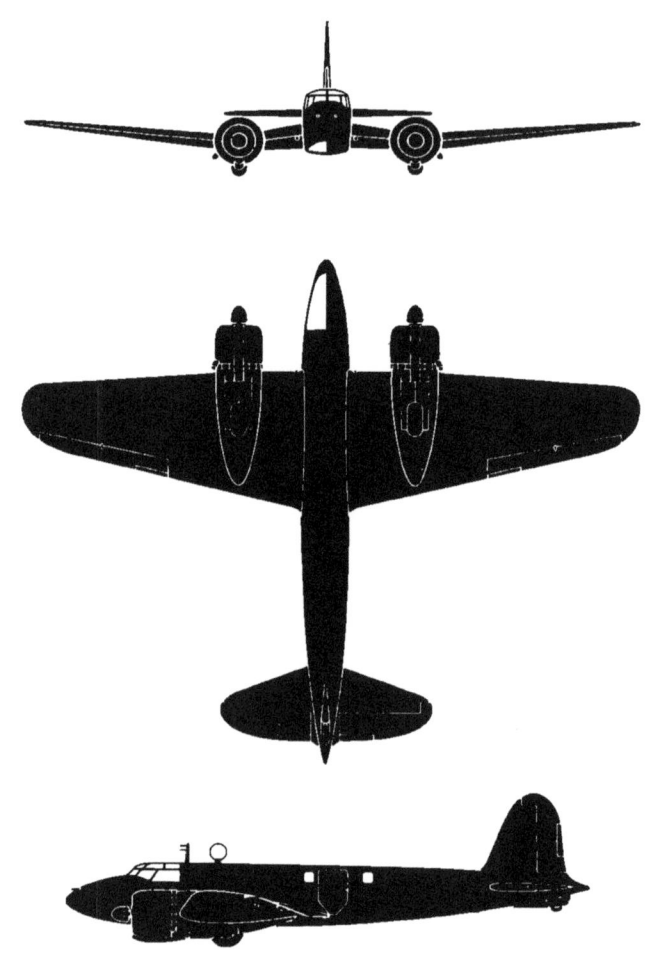

FIAT C.R. 25 (2—Fiat)
Bomber Reconnaissance

Span 51′ 10″ Length 44′ 3″

JULY 1943 — ITALY 208

CR 25

TWIN-ENGINE BOMBER

Mfr.: FIAT. Crew: THREE.
Duty: BOMBING. GROUND ATTACK. RECONNAISSANCE.

PERFORMANCE

Max. speed __285__ m.p.h. at __15,000__ ft. altitude; 250 mph at sea level.

Cruising speed: normal __245__ m.p.h.; economical __175__ m.p.h.; at __15,000__ ft. altitude.

Climb: to __15,000__ ft. altitude in __9.5__ min.

Fuel: normal __422__ U.S. gals.; max. _____ U.S. gals.

Service ceiling: normal load __28,500__ ft.; max. bomb/fuel load _____ ft.; min. fuel/no bombs __32,000__ ft.

RANGES

Speeds	With Normal Fuel/Bomb Load	With Max. Bomb Load	With Max. Fuel Load
Normal cruising	1,075 miles	800 miles	_____ miles
Economical cruising	1,360 miles	1,010 miles	_____ miles

POWER PLANT

Number of motors __2__ Rated __840__ horsepower each at __12,500__ ft. altitude.

Description: Fiat A.74 RC.38, 14 cyl., twin-row, air-cooled radial.

Propellers: 3-blade, Fiat-Hamilton, constant speed.

Superchargers: _____

Misc.: Long chord cowlings with controllable gills.

ARMAMENT

(F - fixed. M - free.)
For'd fuselage: 2 x 12.7 mm or 4 x 7.7 mm (F)
For'd wings: _____
Through hub: _____
Dorsal: 1 x 12.7 mm (M)
Lateral: _____
Ventral: Possibly 1x12.7mm(M)
Tail: _____

BOMB/FREIGHT LOAD

Normal bomb load: __660__ lbs.
Max. bomb load: _____ lbs.
Typical bomb stowage: _____
Alternate bomb stowage: 3 x 220 lbs.
_____ lbs.
Freight and/or troops: _____ lbs.

ARMOR

Frontal: _____
Windshield: _____
Pilot's seat: _____
Dorsal: _____
Lateral: _____
Ventral: _____
Bulkhead: _____
Engine: _____

SPECIFICATIONS

Materials: Steel tube, metal covering. Duralumin.

Span: __55'-1"__ Length: __44'-4"__ Height: __11'-2"__ Wing Area: (gross) 430 sq.ft.

Weights: landing __11,600__ lbs.; normal load __14,200__ lbs.; max. load _____ lbs.

Misc.: Wing of all-metal, two spar construction. Fuselage of steel tube framework with sheet metal covering.

ADDITIONAL TECHNICAL DATA

Top turret believed retractable. Current version may have Fiat A.76 RC.40 engines of 1000 hp each at 13,000 ft.; performance would be improved thereby.

ITALY	P 108	JULY
209		1943

P 108

DESCRIPTION

The P 108 is the only operational four-engine bomber in the I.A.F. It resembles, to a certain extent, the earlier models of the U.S. B-17. Current belief is that the number of these aircraft in service is small.

This aircraft is a four-engine, low-wing monoplane. Wings taper sharply, more so on trailing than leading edges; tips are rounded. There is a single fin and rudder. Inboard engine nacelles project further forward than outboard. Landing gear retracts rearward into nacelles.

| JULY 1943 | P 108 | ITALY 209 |

FOUR-ENGINE BOMBER

Mfr.: **PIAGGIO** Crew: **TEN**

Duty: **BOMBING. TRANSPORT. POSSIBLY TORPEDO-DROPPING.**

PERFORMANCE

Max. speed **270** m.p.h. at **13,000** ft. altitude; 235 mph at sea level (est.)

Cruising speed: normal **230** m.p.h.; economical **190** m.p.h.; at **13,000** ft. altitude. (est.)

Climb: to **13,000** ft. altitude in **16.25** min. (est.)

Fuel: normal (est) **1200** U.S. gals.; max. **1,980** U.S. gals.

Service ceiling: normal load **23,000** ft.; max. bomb/fuel load _____ ft.; min. fuel/no bombs **30,000** ft. (est.)

RANGES

Speeds	With Normal Fuel/Bomb Load	With Max. Bomb Load	With Max. Fuel Load
Normal cruising	(est) 1,550 miles	(est) 900 miles	miles
Economical cruising	(est) 1,700 miles	(est) 990 miles	miles

POWER PLANT

Number of motors **4** Rated **1,300** horsepower each at **11,500** ft. altitude.

Description: **Piaggio P.XII RC.35, 18 cyl., twin-row, air-cooled radial.**

Propellers: **3-blade, Piaggio, constant speed.**

Superchargers:

Misc.: **Long-chord cowlings with controllable gills.**

ARMAMENT

(F - fixed. M - free.)

For'd fuselage: **2 x 12.7mm (M)** in turret.
wings: **4 x 12.7mm (M)**
Through hub:
Dorsal:
Lateral: **2 x 7.7 mm. (M)**
Ventral: **1/2 x 12.7 mm. (M)**
Tail:

BOMB/FREIGHT LOAD

Normal bomb load: (est) **7,700** lbs.
Max. bomb load: (est) **10,000** lbs.
Typical bomb stowage:

7 x 1,100 lbs.
Alternate bomb stowage:

20 x 220 lbs.
Freight and/or troops: _____ lbs.

ARMOR

Frontal: **Some protection**
Windshield:
Pilot's seat: **Both pilots, above, below, behind, 7 mm.**
Dorsal:
Lateral:
Ventral:
Bulkhead:
Self-sealing fuel tanks.
Engine:

SPECIFICATIONS

Materials: **All metal.**

Span: **106'** Length: **73'-6"** Height: _____ Wing Area: (gross) **1,460** sq.ft

Weights: landing **39,500** lbs.; normal load **57,000** lbs.; max. load _____ lbs.

Misc.:

ADDITIONAL TECHNICAL DATA

Each outboard engine nacelle houses two remotely-controlled guns, sighted from transparent dome on the fuselage.

| ITALY 210 | SM 79 | JULY 1943 |

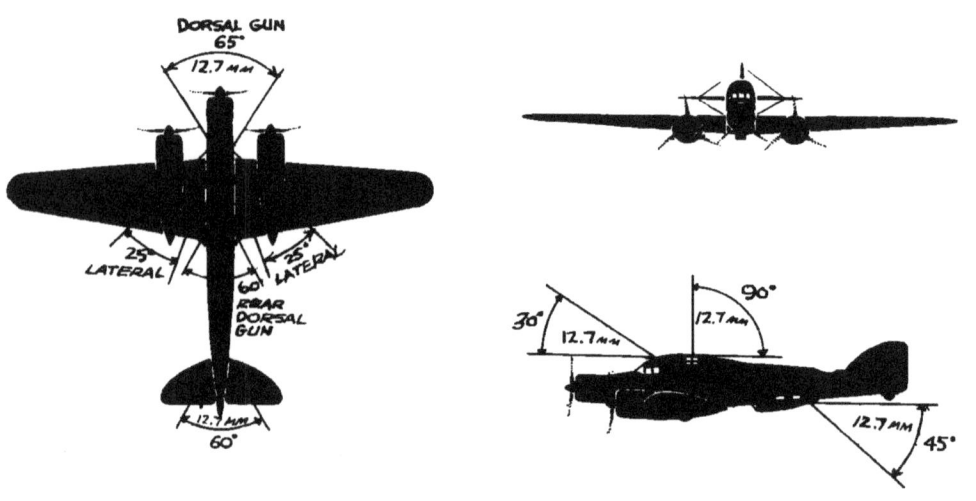

SM 79

DESCRIPTION

The SM 79 is the mainstay of the I.A.F. bomber units. It has been used extensively in anti-shipping activities as a torpedo-bomber. Substantial numbers remain in service.

This aircraft is a three-engine, low-wing monoplane. Wings have straight taper to rounded tips. Trailing edges are hinged, inner sections act as camber-changing flaps, outer sections as ailerons and flaps. Outer section of leading edge has Handley Page slots. There is a single fin and rudder and braced stabilizer. Fuselage is humped behind the cockpit. Rear ventral bombardier's position creates a bulge. Landing gear retracts rearward into nacelles.

| JULY 1943 | SM 79 | ITALY 210 |

THREE-ENGINE BOMBER "SPARVIERO" (HAWK)

Mfr.: **SAVOIA-MARCHETTI** Crew: **FOUR to FIVE**

Duty: **BOMBING, RECONNAISSANCE, TORPEDO-DROPPING.**

PERFORMANCE

Max. speed **255** m.p.h. at **12,500** ft. altitude; 218 mph at sea level.

Cruising speed: normal **211** m.p.h.; economical **192** m.p.h.; at **10,000** ft. altitude.

Climb: to **10,000** ft. altitude in **10.25** min. (normal load); in 14.3 min. (with max. load)

Fuel: normal **888** U.S. gals.; max. **1344** U.S. gals.

Service ceiling: normal load **23,000** ft.; max. bomb/fuel load **19,500** ft.; min. fuel/no bombs **28,000** ft.

RANGES

Speeds	With Normal Fuel/Bomb Load	With Max. Bomb Load (and 984 gals.)	With Max. Fuel Load (see "Specifications")
Normal cruising	1,510 miles	1,650 miles	2,310 miles
Economical cruising	1,630 miles	1,760 miles	2,470 miles

POWER PLANT

Number of motors **3** Rated **750** horsepower each at **11,000** ft. altitude.

Description: **Alfa-Romeo 126 RC.34, 9 cyl., air-cooled radial.**

Propellers: **3-blade, metal, variable pitch, Alfa-Romeo, c.s.**

Superchargers:

Misc.: **Long-chord cowlings.**

ARMAMENT
(F - fixed. M - free.)

For'd fuselage:
For'd wings:
Through hub:
Dorsal: **2x12.7mm(M) 350/500 rds**
Lateral: **2x12.7mm(M) 500 r.p.g.**
Ventral: **1x12.7mm(M) 500 rds.**
Tail:

BOMB/FREIGHT LOAD

Normal bomb load: **2,750** lbs.
Max. bomb load: **2,940** lbs.
Typical bomb stowage:
  5 x 550 lbs.
Alternate bomb stowage: 12 x 220 lbs.
  2 x 1100 lbs.
  .48 x33 or 90 x 26 lbs.
(est.) 1/2 Torpedoes, **1100** lbs.
Freight and/or troops: _____ lbs.

ARMOR

Frontal:
Windshield:
Pilot's seat: **5-8 mm.**
Dorsal: **8 mm.**
Lateral: **5 mm.**
Ventral: **5 mm.**
Bulkhead:
Engine:

SPECIFICATIONS

Materials: **Metal, plywood, fabric.**

Span: **69'-6"** Length: **51'** Height: **15'-1"** Wing Area: (gross) **664 sq.ft.**

Weights: landing **17,500** lbs.; normal load **23,070** lbs.; max. load **26,700** lbs.

Misc.: **When overloaded with fuel to about 30,800 lbs. a range of 3,750 miles might be obtained.**

ADDITIONAL TECHNICAL DATA

All guns (except forward of fuselage gun) are on manually-operated mountings. Fixed gun sometimes omitted.

ITALY — SM 84 bis — ITALY
211 — 1943

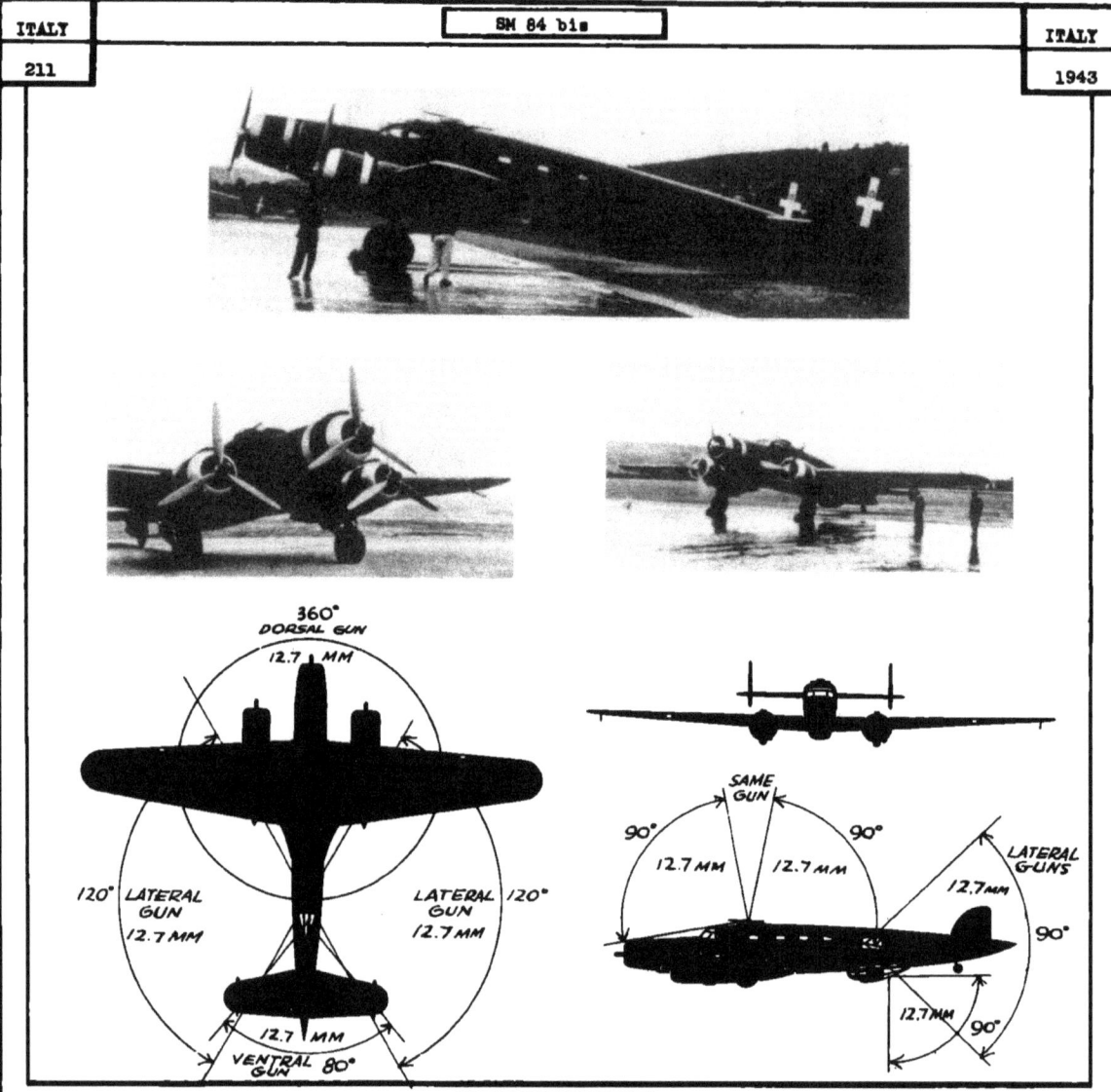

SM 84 bis

DESCRIPTION

The SM 84 was developed from the SM 79 which it probably was intended to supersede. Indications are, however, that the aircraft is not very popular and only a limited number appear to be in service.

This aircraft is a three-engine, low-wing monoplane. Wings have a straight taper to rounded tips. Trailing edges are hinged; inner sections act as camber-changing flaps and outer sections as ailerons and flaps. There are twin fins and rudders; stabilizer is braced. Ventral bombardier's position creates bulge under rear fuselage. Landing gear retracts rearward into nacelles.

| JULY 1943 | | SM 84 bis | | ITALY 211 |

THREE-ENGINE BOMBER

Mfr.: SAVOIA-MARCHETTI   Crew: FOUR to FIVE
Duty: BOMBING, RECONNAISSANCE, TORPEDO-BOMBING,

PERFORMANCE

Max. speed 290 m.p.h. at 15,000 ft. altitude; 253 mph at sea level (est.)

Cruising speed: normal 250 m.p.h.; economical 200 m.p.h.; at 15,000 ft. altitude. (est)

Climb: to 15,000 ft. altitude in 17 min. (est)

Fuel: normal (est) 672 U.S. gals.; max. 861 U.S. gals.

Service ceiling: normal load 24,000 ft.; max. bomb/fuel load _____ ft.; min. fuel/no bombs 29,500 ft.
(est)   (est)

RANGES

Speeds	With Normal Fuel/Bomb Load	With Max. Bomb Load	With Max. Fuel Load
Normal cruising	950 miles	miles	1,285 miles
Economical cruising	1,040 miles	miles	1,400 miles

POWER PLANT

Number of motors 3 Rated 1000 horsepower each at 13,200 ft. altitude.

Description: Piaggio P.XI bis RC. 40D, 14 cyl., twin-row, air-cooled radial,

Propellers: 3-blade, metal, Piaggio, constant speed, variable pitch,

Superchargers:

Misc.: Long-chord cowlings with controllable gills,

ARMAMENT

(F - fixed. M - free.)
For'd fuselage:
For'd wings:
Through hub:
Dorsal: 1 x 12.7 mm (M)
Lateral: 2x12.7mm(M) 630 rpg
Ventral: 1x12.7mm(M) 350 rds.
Tail:

BOMB/FREIGHT LOAD

Normal bomb load: _____ lbs.
Max. bomb load: 5,830 lbs.
Typical bomb stowage:
  5 x 550 and 14 x 220 lbs.
Alternate bomb stowage:
  3 x 1100 lbs.
Torpedoes, 2 x 1760 lbs.
Freight and/or troops:
  _____ lbs.

ARMOR

Frontal:
Windshield:
Pilot's seat: Back, head, sides of both seats, 6-9 mm.
Dorsal Turret top, sides 9-10mm
Lateral On, below guns, 6-8mm
Ventral On gun, bola floor, 8mm
Bulkhead:
Engine:

SPECIFICATIONS

Materials: Metal, plywood, fabric.

Span: 69'-4"   Length: 60'   Height: _____   Wing Area: (gross) 648 sq.ft.

Weights: landing 21,000 lbs.; normal load 27,700 lbs.; max. load _____ lbs.

Misc.:

ADDITIONAL TECHNICAL DATA

Gun balancing rod in dorsal turret gives impression of a second gun.

DESCRIPTION

A.L. 24 to A.P. 1480 C (Section B) RO 57

RO 57 (2—Fiat)
Dive Bomber

Span 47' 6" Length 32' 0"

Provisional Silhouette

Mfr.:_____ Crew:_____
Duty:_____

PERFORMANCE

Max. speed_____ m.p.h. at_____ ft. altitude.

Cruising speed: normal_____ m.p.h.; economical_____ m.p.h.; at_____ ft. altitude.

Climb: to_____ ft. altitude in_____ min. _____

Fuel: normal_____ U.S. gals.; max._____ U.S. gals. _____

Service ceiling: normal load_____ ft.; max. bomb/fuel load_____ ft.; min. fuel/no bombs_____ ft.

RANGES

Speeds	With Normal Fuel/Bomb Load	With Max. Bomb Load	With Max. Fuel Load
Normal cruising	_____ miles	_____ miles	_____ miles
Economical cruising	_____ miles	_____ miles	_____ miles

POWER PLANT

Number of motors_____ Rated_____ horsepower each at_____ ft. altitude.

Description:_____

Propellers:_____

Superchargers:_____

Misc.:_____

ARMAMENT

(F - fixed. M - free.)

For'd fuselage:_____
For'd wings:_____
Through hub:_____
Dorsal:_____
Lateral:_____
Ventral:_____
Tail:_____

BOMB/FREIGHT LOAD

Normal bomb load:_____ lbs.
Max. bomb load:_____ lbs.
Typical bomb stowage:_____
_____ lbs.
Alternate bomb stowage:
_____ lbs.
Freight and/or troops:
_____ lbs.

ARMOR

Frontal:_____
Windshield:_____
Pilot's seat:___
Dorsal:_____
Lateral:_____
Ventral:_____
Bulkhead:_____
Engine:_____

SPECIFICATIONS

Materials:_____

Span:_____ Length:_____ Height:_____ Wing Area:_____

Weights: landing_____ lbs.; normal load_____ lbs.; max. load_____ lbs.

Misc.:_____

ADDITIONAL TECHNICAL DATA

_____
_____
_____

ITALY	G 12	JULY
301		1943

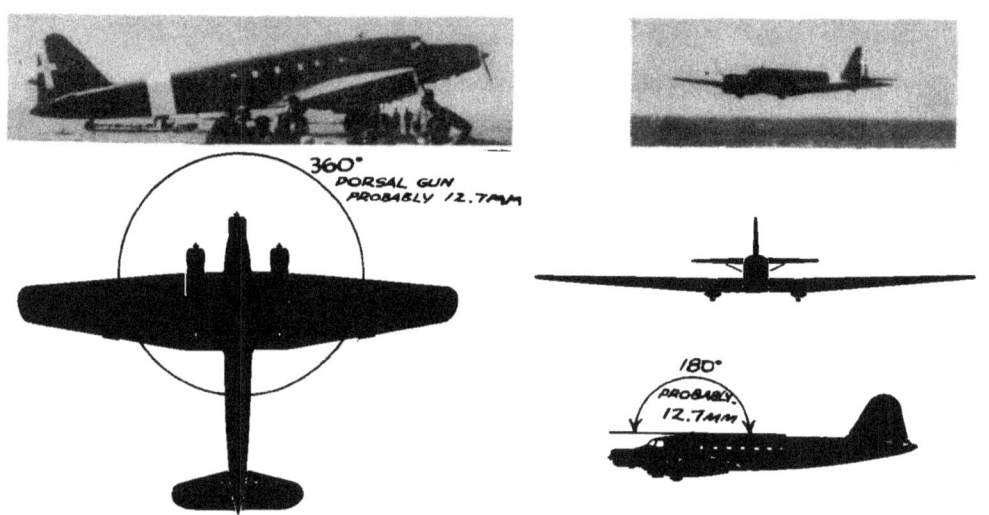

G 12

DESCRIPTION

The G 12 is a transport in limited use by the I.A.F.

It is a three-engine, low-wing monoplane. Wing center section is parallel in chord; outer sections are tapered. Split flaps are fitted. Fuselage is parallel-sided with rounded top. There is a single fin and rudder with a braced stabilizer. Landing gear retracts forward into engine nacelles.

JULY 1943 | **G 12** | ITALY 301

THREE-ENGINE TRANSPORT

Mfr.: FIAT. Crew: FOUR.
Duty: TRANSPORT.

PERFORMANCE

Max. speed 245 m.p.h. at 15,000 ft. altitude; 220 mph at sea level. (est.)

Cruising speed: normal 213 m.p.h.; economical 155 m.p.h.; at 15,000 ft. altitude.(est.)

Climb: to 15,000 ft. altitude in 15.5 min. (est.)

Fuel: normal 699 U.S. gals.; max. 765 U.S. gals.

Service ceiling: normal load 27,500 ft.; max. bomb/fuel load ___ ft.; min. fuel/no bombs 32,500 ft.
(est.) (est.)

RANGES

Speeds	With Normal Fuel/Bomb Load	With Max. Bomb Load	With Max. Fuel Load (1,600 lbs.)
Normal cruising	(est.) 875 miles	___ miles	(est.) 1,240 miles
Economical cruising	(est.) 1,110 miles	___ miles	(est.) 1,585 miles

POWER PLANT

Number of motors 3 Rated 770 horsepower each at 13,750 ft. altitude.

Description: Fiat A.74 RC.42, 14 cyl., twin-row, air-cooled radial.

Propellers: 3-blade, Fiat-Hamilton, constant speed.

Superchargers:

Misc.: Nose and wing engines have long chord magni cowlings with controllable gills.

ARMAMENT

(F - fixed. M - free.)
For'd fuselage:
For'd wings:
Through hub:
Dorsal: Probably 1x12.7mm (M)
Lateral:
Ventral:
Tail:

BOMB/FREIGHT LOAD

Normal bomb load: ___ lbs.
Max. bomb load: ___ lbs.
Typical bomb stowage: ___ lbs.

Alternate bomb stowage: ___ lbs.

Freight and/or troops: ___ lbs.
3,075 lbs.

ARMOR

Frontal:
Windshield:
Pilot's seat:
Dorsal:
Lateral:
Ventral:
Bulkhead:
Engine:

SPECIFICATIONS

Materials: Metal stressed skin fabric.

Span: 94' Length: 66' Height: 16' Wing Area: (gross) 1,216 sq.ft

Weights: landing 21,100 lbs.; normal load 27,500 lbs.; max. load (est.) 34,100 lbs.

Misc.:

ADDITIONAL TECHNICAL DATA

With overload of fuel range may approximate 2500 miles.

ITALY	Ro 37 bis	JULY
302		1943

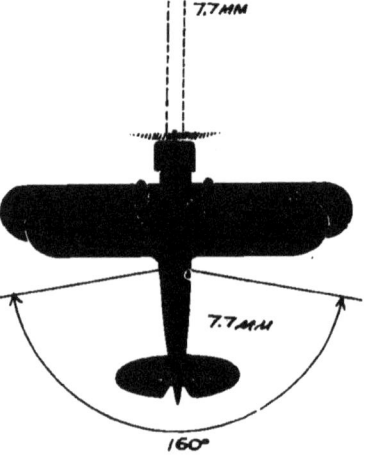

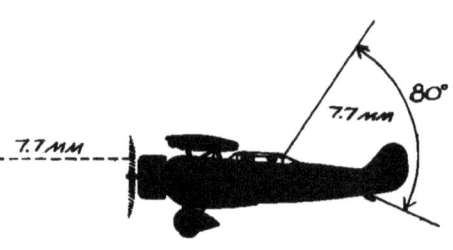

Ro 37 bis

DESCRIPTION

The Ro 37 bis army cooperation aircraft still seems to be in limited use.

The aircraft is a single-engine biplane. Wings are of unequal span, the top one the longer of the two. They are slightly staggered. Ailerons are on upper wing only. Center section of top wing braced by "N" struts to fuselage. Landing gear is fixed; wheel fairings are fitted. Open cockpits are placed behind the top wing's trailing edge.

JULY 1943 | Ro 37 bis | ITALY 302

SINGLE-ENGINE ARMY COOPERATION

Mfr.: MERIDIONALI.　　　　　Crew: TWO.
Duty: ARMY COOPERATION.

PERFORMANCE

Max. speed __200__ m.p.h. at __15,000__ ft. altitude; 178 mph at sea level.

Cruising speed: normal __172__ m.p.h.; economical __125__ m.p.h.; at __15,000__ ft. altitude.

Climb: to __15,000__ ft. altitude in __10.25__ min.

Fuel: normal __112__ U.S. gals.; max. __174__ U.S. gals.

Service ceiling: normal load __25,500__ ft.; max. bomb/fuel load _____ ft.; min. fuel/no bombs __30,000__ ft.

RANGES

Speeds	With Normal Fuel/Bomb Load	With Max. Bomb Load	With Max. Fuel Load
Normal cruising	550 miles	____ miles	940 miles
Economical cruising	740 miles	____ miles	1,190 miles

POWER PLANT

Number of motors __1__　Rated __560__ horsepower each at __13,100__ ft. altitude.

Description: Piaggio P.IX RC.40, 9 cyl., air-cooled radial.

Propellers: 3-blade, metal, Piaggio, adjustable pitch.

Superchargers:

Misc.: Long chord cowling.

ARMAMENT

(F - fixed. M - free.)

For'd fuselage: 2 x 7.7mm (F)
For'd wings:
Through hub:
Dorsal: 1 x 7.7mm (M)
Lateral:
Ventral:
Tail:

BOMB/FREIGHT LOAD

Normal bomb load: _____ lbs.
Max. bomb load: 400 lbs.
Typical bomb stowage:

　　12 x 33 lbs.
Alternate bomb stowage:

　　_____ lbs.
Freight and/or troops:
　　_____ lbs.

ARMOR

Frontal:
Windshield:
Pilot's seat:
Dorsal:
Lateral:
Ventral:
Bulkhead:
Engine:

SPECIFICATIONS

Materials: Metal, wood, fabric.

Span: 36'-4"　　Length: 28'-2"　　Height: 10'-2"　　Wing Area: (gross) 338 sq.ft.

Weights: landing __4,200__ lbs.; normal load __5,300__ lbs.; max. load _____ lbs.

Misc.: Metal spars and wooden ribs.

ADDITIONAL TECHNICAL DATA

| ITALY 303 | SM 75 | JULY 1943 |

SM 75

DESCRIPTION

The SM 75 is one of the older, obsolete transports of the I.A.F. which is still in operation.

The aircraft is a three-engine, low-wing monoplane. Wing has straight taper to rounded tips. Trailing edges are hinged; inner sections act as camber-changing flap and outer sections as ailerons and flaps. Outer section of leading edges are fitted with Handley Page slots. There is a single fin and rudder and a braced stabilizer. Cockpit is over the leading edges. Landing gear retracts rearward into engine nacelles.

| JULY 1943 | | SM 75 | | ITALY 303 |

THREE-ENGINE TRANSPORT "MARSUPIALE" (MARSUPIAL)

Mfr.: SAVOIA-MARCHETTI.　　　　　　　　Crew: FOUR to FIVE.
Duty: TRANSPORT.

PERFORMANCE

Max. speed 212 m.p.h. at 13,000 ft. altitude; 190 mph at sea level.

Cruising speed: normal 178 m.p.h.; economical 150 m.p.h.; at 13,000 ft. altitude.

Climb: to 13,000 ft. altitude in 18.5 min.

Fuel: normal (est.) 977 U.S. gals.; max. _____ U.S. gals.

Service ceiling: normal load 22,500 ft.; max. bomb/fuel load _____ ft.; min. fuel/no bombs 29,500 ft.

RANGES

Speeds	With Normal Fuel/Bomb Load (3,400 lbs. load)	With Max. Bomb Load (346 gals.)	With Max. Fuel Load
Normal cruising	1,370 miles	425 miles	_____ miles
Economical cruising	1,485 miles	458 miles	_____ miles

POWER PLANT

Number of motors 3　　Rated 750 horsepower each at 11,150 ft. altitude.

Description: Alfa-Romeo 126 RC.34, 9 cyl., air-cooled radial.

Propellers:
Superchargers:
Misc.:

ARMAMENT

(F - fixed. M - free.)

For'd fuselage:
For'd wings:
Through hub:
Dorsal:
Lateral:
Ventral:
Tail:

BOMB/FREIGHT LOAD

Normal bomb load: _____ lbs.
Max. bomb load: _____ lbs.
Typical bomb stowage: _____
_____ lbs.
Alternate bomb stowage:
_____ lbs.
Freight and/or troops: 7,800 lbs.

ARMOR

Frontal:
Windshield:
Pilot's seat:
Dorsal:
Lateral:
Ventral:
Bulkhead:
Engine:

SPECIFICATIONS

Materials: Metal, plywood, fabric.

Span: 97'-5"　　Length: 73'-1"　　Height: 17'-4"　　Wing Area (gross) 1,276 sq.ft

Weights: landing 22,000 lbs.; normal load 32,000 lbs.; max. load _____ lbs.

Misc.: Wing of three spars, solid plywood ribs and plywood skin, all fabric covered. Fuselage of welded steel tube structure.

ADDITIONAL TECHNICAL DATA

Reported that this type has been converted for use as a bomber.

3-7114, AP

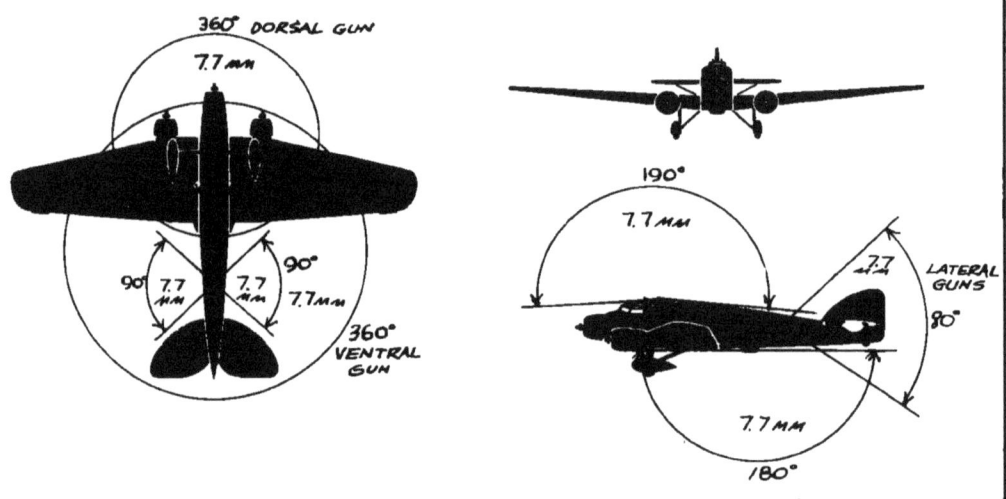

DESCRIPTION

The SM 81 is an obsolete bomber used primarily as a transport by the I.A.F.

The aircraft is a three-engine, low-wing monoplane. Wing center section is approximately parallel in chord, outer sections tapering to round tips. Variable-camber flaps are fitted. There is a single fin and rudder with a braced stabilizer. Cockpit is forward of the leading edge. Bombardier's compartment behind the nose engine is semi-retractable. The landing gear is fixed.

JULY 1943 — ITALY 304

SM 81

THREE-ENGINE TRANSPORT-BOMBER "PIPISTRELLO" (BAT)

Mfr.: SAVOIA-MARCHETTI. Crew: FOUR to FIVE.
Duty: TRANSPORT. BOMBING.

PERFORMANCE

Max. speed 210 m.p.h. at 14,000 ft. altitude; 188 mph at sea level.
Cruising speed: normal 181 m.p.h.; economical 140 m.p.h.; at 14,000 ft. altitude.
Climb: to 14,000 ft. altitude in 14.7 min.
Fuel: normal 687 U.S. gals.; max. 958 U.S. gals.
Service ceiling: normal load _____ ft.; max. bomb/fuel load _____ ft.; min. fuel/no bombs _____ ft.

RANGES

Speeds	With Normal Fuel/Bomb Load	With Max. Bomb Load (337 gals.)	With Max. Fuel Load
Normal cruising	1,035 miles	485 miles	1,475 miles
Economical cruising	1,240 miles	580 miles	1,770 miles

POWER PLANT

Number of motors 3 Rated 700 horsepower each at 14,000 ft. altitude.
Description: Alfa Romeo 125 RC.35, 9 cyl., air-cooled radial.
Propellers: 3-blade, metal, fixed pitch.
Superchargers:
Misc.: Alternative engines are Piaggio PXR, Piaggio PIXR or Gnome Rhone K.14.

ARMAMENT

(F - fixed. M - free.)
For'd fuselage:
For'd wings:
Through hub:
Dorsal: 2 x 7.7 mm (M)
Lateral: 2 x 7.7 mm (M)
Ventral: 2 x 7.7 mm (M)
Tail:

BOMB/FREIGHT LOAD

Normal bomb load: 2,200 lbs.
Max. bomb load: 4,400 lbs.
Typical bomb stowage: 4 x 550 lbs.
Alternate bomb stowage: 4 x 1100 lbs.
16 x 220 lbs.
Torpedoes, 2 x 1760 lbs.
Freight and/or troops: 20 Troops _____ lbs.

ARMOR

Frontal:
Windshield:
Pilot's seat:
Dorsal:
Lateral:
Ventral:
Bulkhead:
Engine:

SPECIFICATIONS

Materials: Wood, metal, fabric.
Span: 79' Length: 59' Height: 15' Wing Area (gross) 1,000 sq.ft
Weights: landing 15,800 lbs.; normal load 22,200 lbs.; max. load _____ lbs.
Misc.: Wing made of three main wooden spars and plywood covering. Fuselage of welded steel tubing with fabric covering.

ADDITIONAL TECHNICAL DATA

Dorsal and ventral turrets power-driven.

ITALY — SM 82 — JULY
305 — 1943

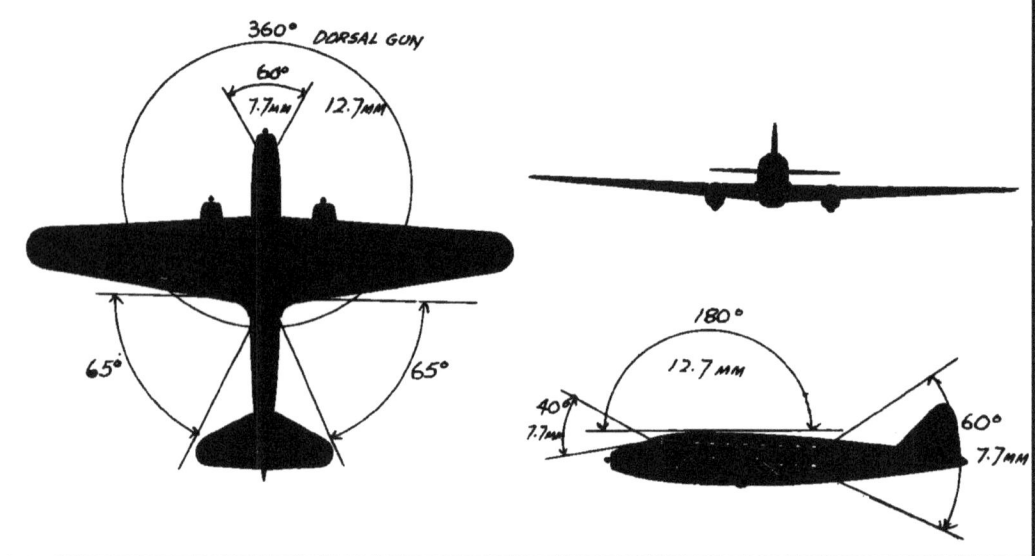

SM 82

DESCRIPTION

The SM 82 makes up the greater part of the I.A.F. transport units. It probably will remain in extensive use.

The aircraft is a three-engine, low-wing monoplane. Wings taper moderately to rounded tips. Handley-Page leading-edge slots are fitted and work automatically, according to air speed, in conjunction with flaps and ailerons. Fuselage is of large cross section. Cockpit is forward of leading edge. There is a single fin and rudder. Landing gear retracts hydraulically.

JULY		ITALY
1943	SM 82	305

THREE-ENGINE TRANSPORT "CANGURU" (KANGAROO)

Mfr.: **SAVOIA-MARCHETTI.** Crew: **FOUR to FIVE.**
Duty: **TRANSPORT.**

PERFORMANCE

Max. speed __205__ m.p.h. at __7,000__ ft. altitude; 185 mph at sea level.

Cruising speed: normal __172__ m.p.h.; economical __155__ m.p.h.; at __10,000__ ft. altitude.

Climb: to __10,000__ ft. altitude in __16.5__ min.

Fuel: normal __928__ U.S. gals.; max. __1,567__ U.S. gals.

Service ceiling: normal load __17,000__ ft.; max. bomb/fuel load _____ ft.; min. fuel/no bombs __20,500__ ft.

RANGES

Speeds	With Normal Fuel/Bomb Load	With Max. Bomb Load	With Max. Fuel Load
Normal cruising	1,160 miles	miles	2,000 miles
Economical cruising	1,250 miles	miles	2,200 miles

POWER PLANT

Number of motors __3__ Rated __860__ horsepower each at __6,900__ ft. altitude.

Description: __Alfa-Romeo 128 RC.21, 9 cyl., air-cooled radial.__

Propellers: __3-blade, metal, constant speed.__

Superchargers:

Misc.: __Long-chord cowlings with controllable gills.__

ARMAMENT
(F - fixed. M - free.)
For'd fuselage: 1 x 7.7mm (M)
For'd wings:
Through hub:
Dorsal: 1 x 12.7mm (M)
Lateral: 2 x 7.7mm (M)
Ventral:
Tail:

BOMB/FREIGHT LOAD
Normal bomb load: _____ lbs.
Max. bomb load: _____ lbs.
Typical bomb stowage:
_____ lbs.
Alternate bomb stowage:
(See below, "Additional Technical Data")
_____ lbs.
Freight and/or troops:
30/35 equipped parachutists ___ lbs.

ARMOR
Frontal:
Windshield:
Pilot's seat:
Dorsal:
Lateral:
Ventral:
Bulkhead:
Engine:

SPECIFICATIONS

Materials: __Wood, metal, fabric.__

Span: __97'-6"__ Length: __73'-6"__ Height: __18'__ Wing Area: (gross) __1,290 sq.ft.__

Weights: landing __34,000__ lbs.; normal load __39,700__ lbs.; max. load _____ lbs.

Misc.: __Wing made of three wooden spars and solid plywood ribs. Plywood skin covered with doped fabric. Fuselage of welded steel tubing.__

ADDITIONAL TECHNICAL DATA

Stated to be capable of carrying following alternative loads: (1) 75 mm gun with ammunition and/or one flame-throwing outfit with crew and equipment. (2) a small tank. (3) 51 men with light automatic weapons. (4) A dismantled CR 42 fighter, which is carried with wings detached and stowed along the sides of the fuselage.

Mfr.: _____ Crew: _____
Duty: _____

PERFORMANCE

Max. speed _____ m.p.h. at _____ ft. altitude.

Cruising speed: normal _____ m.p.h.; economical _____ m.p.h.; at _____ ft. altitude.

Climb: to _____ ft. altitude in _____ min. _____

Fuel: normal _____ U.S. gals.; max. _____ U.S. gals. _____

Service ceiling: normal load _____ ft.; max. bomb/fuel load _____ ft.; min. fuel/no bombs _____ ft.

RANGES

Speeds	With Normal Fuel/Bomb Load	With Max. Bomb Load	With Max. Fuel Load
Normal cruising	_____ miles	_____ miles	_____ miles
Economical cruising	_____ miles	_____ miles	_____ miles

POWER PLANT

Number of motors _____ Rated _____ horsepower each at _____ ft. altitude.

Description: _____

Propellers: _____

Superchargers: _____

Misc.: _____

ARMAMENT | BOMB/FREIGHT LOAD | ARMOR

(F - fixed. M - free.)

For'd fuselage: _____
For'd wings: _____
Through hub: _____
Dorsal: _____
Lateral: _____
Ventral: _____
Tail: _____

Normal bomb load: _____ lbs.
Max. bomb load: _____ lbs.
Typical bomb stowage: _____
_____ lbs.
Alternate bomb stowage:
_____ lbs.
Freight and/or troops:
_____ lbs.

Frontal: _____
Windshield: _____
Pilot's seat: _____
Dorsal: _____
Lateral: _____
Ventral: _____
Bulkhead: _____
Engine: _____

SPECIFICATIONS

Materials: _____

Span: _____ Length: _____ Height: _____ Wing Area: _____

Weights: landing _____ lbs.; normal load _____ lbs.; max. load _____ lbs.

Misc.: _____

ADDITIONAL TECHNICAL DATA

_____
_____
_____

| ITALY | Ca 312 bis, I.S. | JULY |
| 401 | | 1943 |

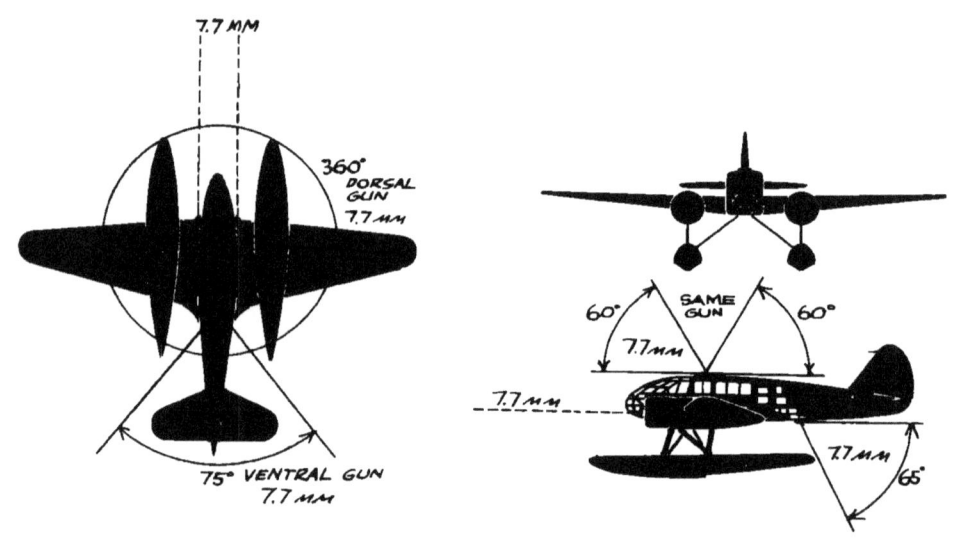

Ca 312 bis, I.S.

DESCRIPTION

The Ca 312 bis or I.S. floatplane was developed from the Ca 311 and Ca 312 bis landplanes. The type is still believed to be in service.

The aircraft is a twin-engine, twin-float, low-wing monoplane. Wing tapers moderately to rounded tips. The blunt nose is almost completely transparent. The sides of the fuselage are fitted with a large amount of transparent panelling. There is a single fin and rudder. Single-step metal floats are attached to the center section by vertical "N" struts and to fuselage by inverted "V" struts.

JULY 1943 — ITALY — 401

Ca 313 bis, I.S.

TWIN-ENGINE FLOATPLANE

Mfr.: **CAPRONI** Crew: **THREE to FOUR**
Duty: **RECONNAISSANCE. BOMBING. TORPEDO-DROPPING (I.S.).**

PERFORMANCE

Max. speed **230** m.p.h. at **13,000** ft. altitude; 208 mph at sea level. (est.)

Cruising speed: normal **194** m.p.h.; economical **150** m.p.h.; at **13,000** ft. altitude. (est.)

Climb: to **13,000** ft. altitude in **12.75** min. (est.)

Fuel: normal (est.) **139** U.S. gals.; max. (est.) **422** U.S. gals.

Service ceiling: normal load **23,000** ft.; max. bomb/fuel load _____ ft.; min. fuel/no bombs **28,000** ft.
(est.) (est.)

RANGES

Speeds	With Normal Fuel/Bomb Load	With Max. Bomb Load	With Max. Fuel Load
Normal cruising	_____ miles	(est.) 310 miles	(est.) 1,090 miles
Economical cruising	_____ miles	(est.) 360 miles	(est.) 1,275 miles

POWER PLANT

Number of motors **2** Rated **640** horsepower each at **11,500** ft. altitude.

Description: **Piaggio P.XVI RC.35, 9 cyl., air-cooled radial.**

Propellers: **3-blade, metal.**

Superchargers: _____

Misc.: **Long-chord cowlings.**

ARMAMENT

(F - fixed. M - free.)
For'd fuselage: _____
For'd wings: **1/2 x 7.7 mm (F)**
Through hub: _____
Dorsal: **Turret, 1 x 7.7 mm (M)**
Lateral: _____
Ventral: **Poss. 1 x 7.7 mm (M)**
Tail: _____

BOMB/FREIGHT LOAD

Normal bomb load: (est.) **880** lbs.
Max. bomb load: **1,760** lbs.
Typical bomb stowage: **Internal**
(est.) **4 x 220** lbs.
Alternate bomb stowage:
(est.) **8 x 110** lbs.
(I.S. model) Torpedo, **1 x 1760** lbs.
Freight and/or troops: _____ lbs.

ARMOR

Frontal: _____
Windshield: _____
Pilot's seat: _____
Dorsal: _____
Lateral: _____
Ventral: _____
Bulkhead: _____
Engine: _____

SPECIFICATIONS

Materials: **Wood, welded steel tube, fabric and plywood covering.**

Span: **53'-4"** Length: **44'** Height: **10'-6"** Wing Area (gross) **417** sq.ft.

Weights: landing (est.) **10,200** lbs.; normal load (est.) **12,800** lbs.; max. load _____ lbs.

Misc.: **Dorsal gun is in manually-operated turret, probably with indirect sighting.**

ADDITIONAL TECHNICAL DATA

Ca 312 I.S. is torpedo-carrying version which is said to be fitted with a streamlined housing for the torpedo.

ITALY	Ca 316	JULY
402		1943

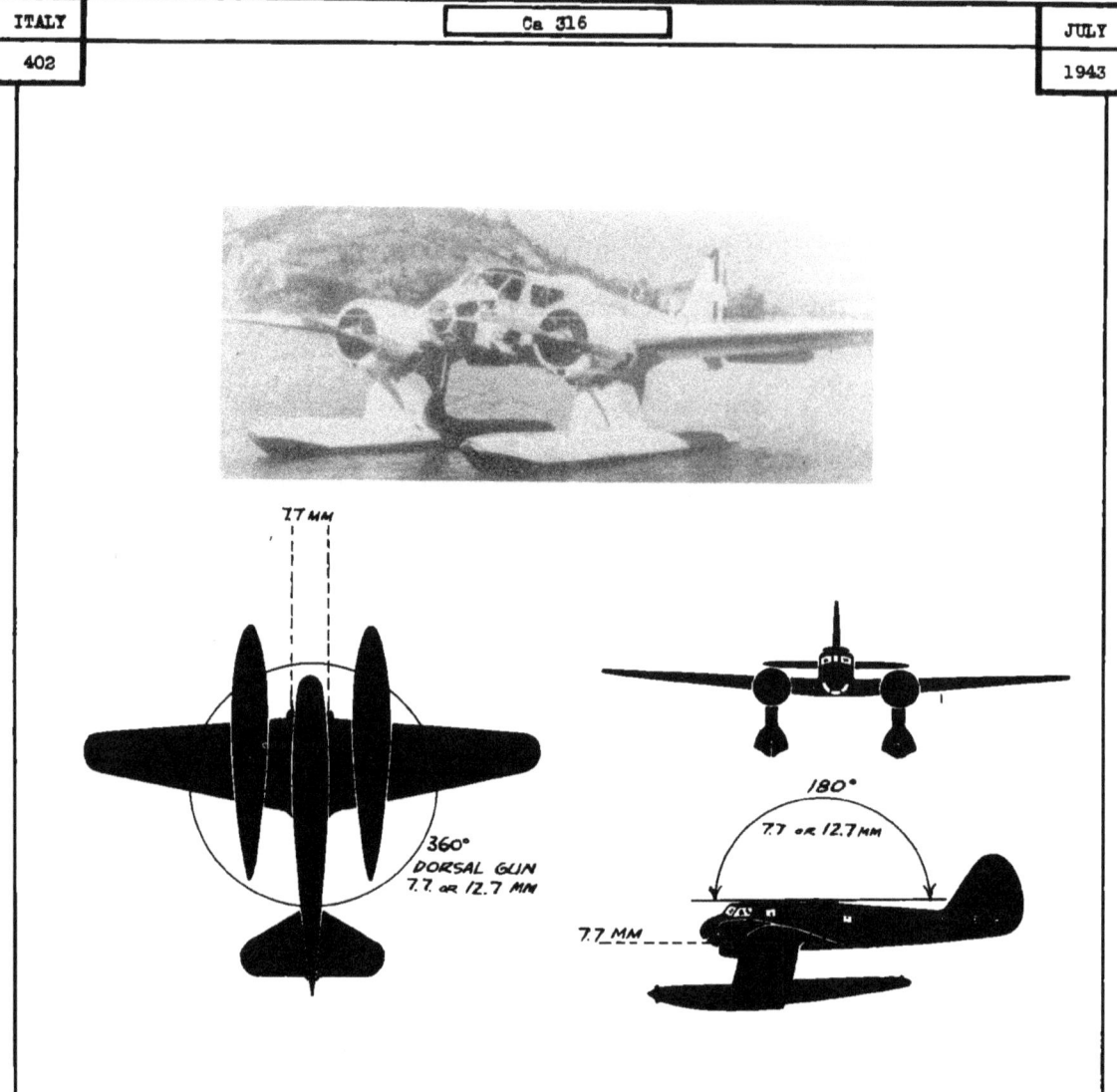

Ca 316

DESCRIPTION

The Ca 316 is a floatplane developed from the Ca 313 landplane and designed especially for catapult operations. It is probably in service in limited numbers.

The aircraft is a twin-engine, twin-float, low-wing monoplane. Wing tapers moderately to rounded tips. The nose is short with transparent panels in tip, lower sections and sides. Additional windows are placed aft of the cockpit. The single fin and rudder is of large area. Stabilizer's leading edges taper sharply. Twin metal floats are supported by large, faired structures.

| JULY 1943 | Ca 316 | ITALY 402 |

TWIN-ENGINE FLOATPLANE

Mfr.: **CAPRONI** Crew: **THREE to FOUR.**
Duty: **RECONNAISSANCE. TORPEDO-DROPPING.**

PERFORMANCE

Max. speed **243** m.p.h. at **13,000** ft. altitude; 220 mph at sea level.

Cruising speed: normal **210** m.p.h.; economical **150** m.p.h.; at **13,000** ft. altitude.

Climb: to **13,000** ft. altitude in **9.5** min. (normal load); in 12.5 min. (with max. load).

Fuel: normal (est.) **283** U.S. gals.; max. (est.) **422** U.S. gals.

Service ceiling: normal load **27,000** ft.; max. bomb/fuel load **24,000** ft.; min. fuel/no bombs **30,000** ft.

RANGES

Speeds	With Normal Fuel/Bomb Load	With Max. Bomb Load (and 139 U.S. gals.)	With Max. Fuel Load
Normal cruising	810 miles	338 miles	1,180 miles
Economical cruising	1,020 miles	400 miles	1,400 miles

POWER PLANT

Number of motors **2** Rated **640** horsepower each at **11,500** ft. altitude.

Description: **Piaggio P.XVI RC.35, 9 cyl., air-cooled radial.**

Propellers: **2-blade, variable pitch, Fiat-Hamilton or Piaggio.**

Superchargers:

Misc.: **Standard version possibly is fitted with Piaggio P.VII C.16 engines of only 460 hp each, lowering max. speed to 195 mph at 5,000 ft. Long chord cowlings of unusual design.**

ARMAMENT
(F - fixed. M - free.)
For'd fuselage:
For'd wings: **2 x 7.7 mm (F)**
Through hub:
Dorsal: **1 x 7.7/12.7 mm (M)**
Lateral:
Ventral:
Tail:

BOMB/FREIGHT LOAD
Normal bomb load (est.) **880** lbs.
Max. bomb load: (est.) **1,760** lbs.
Typical bomb stowage: _____ lbs.
Alternate bomb stowage:
(est.) Torpedo, **1 x 1760** lbs.
Freight and/or troops: _____ lbs.

ARMOR
Frontal:
Windshield:
Pilot's seat:
Dorsal:
Lateral:
Ventral:
Bulkhead:
Engine:

SPECIFICATIONS

Materials: **Steel tubing, wood, plywood, fabric.**

Span: **53'-2"** Length: **45'** Height: _____ Wing Area: (gross) **416** sq.ft.

Weights: landing **9,250** lbs.; normal load (est.) **11,000** lbs.; max. load (est.) **12,500** lbs.

Misc.: **Stressed for catapulting, with weight limitation in such operations of 11,000 lbs.**

ADDITIONAL TECHNICAL DATA

Dorsal turret is unusually flat, sighting is probably done by a reflector system.

ITALY	Cant Z 501	JULY
403		1943

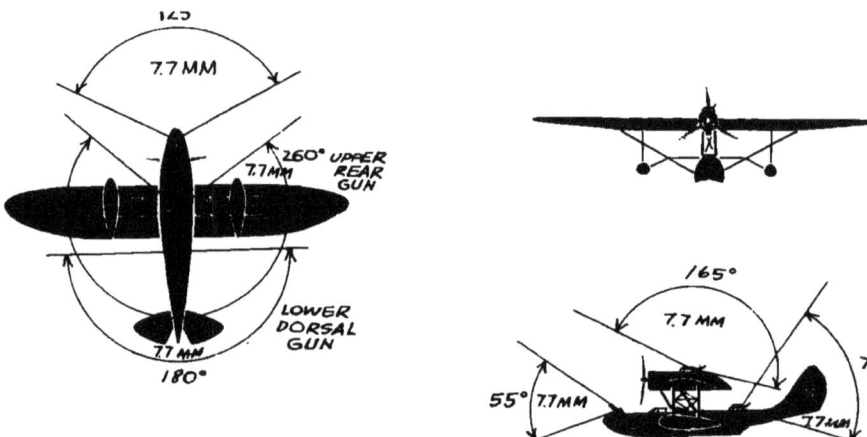

Cant Z 501

DESCRIPTION

The Cant Z 501 is an old-type flying boat that appears to still be operational in limited numbers.

The aircraft is a single-engine, parasol-wing monoplane flying boat. Wing is mainly parallel in chord and braced to hull by parallel struts and mounted above hull on parallel struts; tips are elliptical in shape. Two-step hull is of comparatively shallow section. Stabilizing floats are fitted under the wing. There is a single fin and rudder, with a high-set, braced stabilizer. Nacelle for engine and gunner is placed above the wing.

| JULY 1943 | Cant Z 501 | ITALY 403 |

SINGLE-ENGINE FLYING BOAT

Mfr.: **CANTIERI RIUNITI**   Crew: **FIVE**
Duty: **RECONNAISSANCE. LIGHT BOMBING.**

PERFORMANCE

Max. speed __155__ m.p.h. at __sea level__ ft. altitude (normal load); 145 mph at sea level (with max. load).
Cruising speed: normal __130__ m.p.h.; economical __100__ m.p.h.; at __5,000__ ft. altitude.
Climb: to __5,000__ ft. altitude in __7.6__ min. (normal load); in 12.15 min. (with max. load).
Fuel: normal __482__ U.S. gals.; max. __865__ U.S. gals.
Service ceiling: normal load __16,000__ ft.; max. bomb/fuel load __11,000__ ft.; min. fuel/no bombs __22,000__ ft.

RANGES

Speeds	With Normal Fuel/Bomb Load	With Max. Bomb Load (and 705 U.S. gals.)	With Max. Fuel Load
Normal cruising	1,500 miles	2,090 miles	2,680 miles
Economical cruising	1,700 miles	2,150 miles	2,850 miles

POWER PLANT

Number of motors __1__ Rated __910__ horsepower each at __sea level__ ft. altitude.
Description: __Isotta-Fraschini Asso 750, 18 cyl., liquid-cooled "V".__
Propellers: __3-blade, metal, variable pitch.__
Superchargers: __None.__
Misc.: __Frontal radiator. Stub exhausts. Isotta Fraschini 12 cyl. liquid-cooled "V" also used.__

ARMAMENT

(F - fixed. M - free.)
For'd fuselage: 1 x 7.7 mm (M)
For'd wings:
Through hub:
Dorsal: 1 x 7.7mm (M) in rear hull. 2 x 7.7mm (M) in engine nacelle.
Tail:

BOMB/FREIGHT LOAD

Normal bomb load: _____ lbs.
Max. bomb load: 1,100 lbs.
Typical bomb stowage: Carriers are fitted to main wing bracing struts.
    4 x 220 lbs.
Alternate bomb stowage:
    2 x 550 lbs.
Freight and/or troops: _____ lbs.

ARMOR

Frontal:
Windshield:
Pilot's seat:
Dorsal:
Lateral:
Ventral:
Bulkhead:
Engine:

SPECIFICATIONS

Materials: __Wood, fabric covering.__
Span: __73'-10"__ Length: __46'-11"__ Height: __14'-6"__ Wing Area: (gross) __668__ sq.ft.
Weights: landing __9,500__ lbs.; normal load __12,500__ lbs.; max. load __15,000__ lbs.
Misc.: __Bottom and sides below water line have double skin with layer of doped fabric between.__

ADDITIONAL TECHNICAL DATA

Rear dorsal and engine nacelle turrets hydraulically-operated. Hole behind pilot's seat on starboard side used for bombsight or camera.

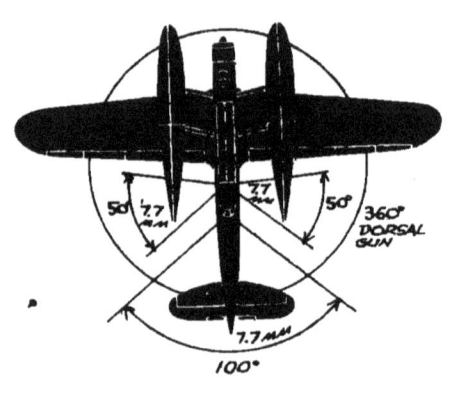
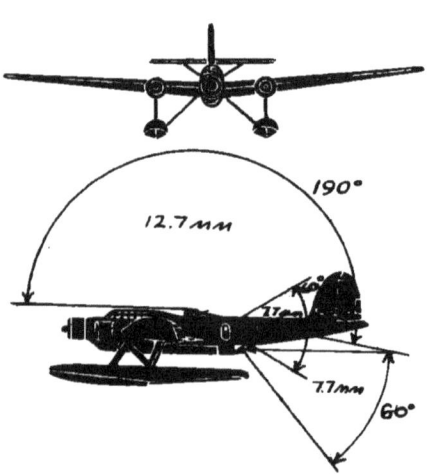

Cant Z 506B

DESCRIPTION

The Cant Z 506B is the principal marine aircraft in use by the I.A.F.

The aircraft is a three-engine, mid-wing, twin-float monoplane. Wing tapers moderately to elliptical tips. Camber-changing flaps and drooping ailerons are fitted. There is a single fin and rudder; the braced stabilizer is mounted on the fin. Pilot's cockpit is forward of the leading edge. Twin, single-step metal floats are attached by struts to the outboard engine mountings and the fuselage.

JULY 1943 — ITALY — 404

Cant Z 506B

THREE-ENGINE FLOATPLANE "AIRONE" (HERON)

Mfr.: CANTIERI RIUNITI **Crew:** FOUR to FIVE

Duty: RECONNAISSANCE. BOMBING. TORPEDO-DROPPING.

PERFORMANCE

Max. speed __230__ m.p.h. at __13,000__ ft. altitude; 196 mph at sea level.

Cruising speed: normal __198__ m.p.h.; economical __147__ m.p.h.; at __13,000__ ft. altitude.

Climb: to __13,000__ ft. altitude in __13__ min.

Fuel: normal __1,095__ U.S. gals.; max.(est.) __1276__ U.S. gals.

Service ceiling: normal load __24,500__ ft.; max. bomb/fuel load __27,500__ ft.; min. fuel/no bombs _____ ft.

RANGES

Speeds	With Normal Fuel/Bomb Load	With Max. Bomb Load (and max. fuel)	With Max. Fuel Load
Normal cruising	1,310 miles	1,665 miles	_____ miles
Economical cruising	1,575 miles	1,915 miles	_____ miles

POWER PLANT

Number of motors __3__ Rated __750__ horsepower each at __11,000__ ft. altitude.

Description: Alfa-Romeo 126 RC.34. 9 cyl., air-cooled radial.

Propellers: 3-blade, metal, Alfa-Romeo, variable pitch, electrically-operated.

Superchargers: _____

Misc.: Long chord cowlings. Compressed air starting: engine driven pump and compressed air bottle. 1 oil tank, capacity 24 U.S. gals., in each engine nacelle.

ARMAMENT

(F - fixed. M - free.)

For'd fuselage: _____
For'd wings: _____
Through hub: _____
Dorsal: Turret.1x12.7mm (M)
Lateral: 2 x 7.7 mm (M)
Ventral: 1 x 7.7 mm (M)
Tail: _____

BOMB/FREIGHT LOAD

Normal bomb load: 1,750 lbs.
Max. bomb load: 2,200 lbs.
Typical bomb stowage: Internal

Alternate bomb stowage:
8 x 220 lbs.
4 x 550 lbs.
20 x 88 lbs.

Freight and/or troops: _____ lbs.

ARMOR

Frontal: _____
Windshield: _____
Pilot's seat: rear pilot. 6mm.
Dorsal: (gunner) 8 mm.
Lateral: _____
Ventral: _____
Bulkhead: _____
Fuel tanks self-sealing.
Engine: _____

SPECIFICATIONS

Materials: Wood, fabric. Metal floats.

Span: 86'-11" Length: 62' Height: 22'-1" Wing Area: (gross) 915 sq.ft.

Weights: landing 23,250 lbs.; normal load 26,750 lbs.; max. load (est.) 29,000 lbs.

Misc.: Wing of wooden structure with three spars and fabric covering. Solid ribs divide wing into water-tight compartments.

ADDITIONAL TECHNICAL DATA

Dorsal gun in a power-driven turret. Four fuel tanks in each wing.

ITALY	Ro 43	JULY
405		1943

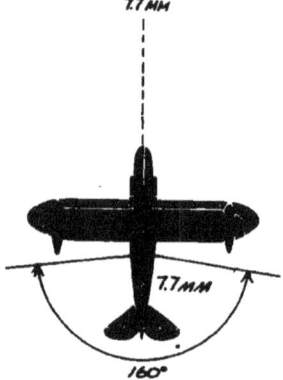

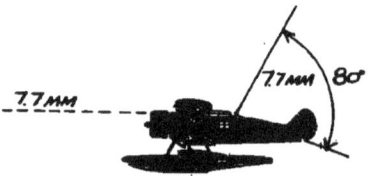

Ro 43

DESCRIPTION

The Ro 43 is an obsolescent floatplane, probably in occasional operation. "Ro" denotes "Romeo", former manufacturer.

It is a single-engine, single-float biplane. Wings are of unequal span designed to fold; top one is the longer. Top and bottom center sections are integral with the fuselage, the former creating a "gulled" effect. Single-step central float attached to fuselage by wire-braced struts. Stabilizing floats of wooden construction are set inboard of lower wing tips. The open cockpits are placed aft of the top wing. Aircraft is stressed for catapulting.

| JULY 1943 | | Ro 43 | | ITALY 405 |

SINGLE-ENGINE FLOATPLANE

Mfr.: **MERIDIONALI**   Crew: **TWO**
Duty: **RECONNAISSANCE**

PERFORMANCE

Max. speed **186** m.p.h. at **8,000** ft. altitude; 180 mph at sea level.
Cruising speed: normal **160** m.p.h.; economical **107** m.p.h.; at **6,500** ft. altitude.
Climb: to **6,500** ft. altitude in **4.3** min.
Fuel: normal **105** U.S. gals.; max. **140** U.S. gals.
Service ceiling: normal load **23,000** ft.; max. bomb/fuel load **22,500** ft.; min. fuel/no bombs **26,000** ft.

RANGES

Speeds	With Normal Fuel/Bomb Load	With Max. Bomb Load	With Max. Fuel Load
Normal cruising	465 miles	miles	630 miles
Economical cruising	650 miles	miles	885 miles

POWER PLANT

Number of motors **1**   Rated **700** horsepower each at **3,300** ft. altitude.
Description: **Piaggio "Stella" PX. RC. 9 cyl., air-cooled radial.**
Propellers: **3-blade, variable pitch.**
Superchargers:
Misc.: **Long chord cowling.**

ARMAMENT

(F - fixed. M - free.)
For'd fuselage: **1 x 7.7mm (F)**
For'd wings:
Through hub:
Dorsal: **1 x 7.7mm (M)**
Lateral:
Ventral:
Tail:

BOMB/FREIGHT LOAD

Normal bomb load: _____ lbs.
Max. bomb load: _____ lbs.
Typical bomb stowage:
_____ lbs.
Alternate bomb stowage:
_____ lbs.
Freight and/or troops: _____ lbs.

ARMOR

Frontal:
Windshield:
Pilot's seat:
Dorsal:
Lateral:
Ventral:
Bulkhead:
Engine:

SPECIFICATIONS

Materials: **Steel tube, wood, fabric.**
Span: **37'-11"**   Length: **31'-10"**   Height: **11'-6"**   Wing Area (gross) **358** sq.ft.
Weights: landing **4,600** lbs.; normal load **5,300** lbs.; max. load **5,500** lbs.
Misc.: **Wings of welded steel tube spars and wooden ribs; outer sections have duralumin spars. Fuselage of steel tubing covered with metal and fabric.**

ADDITIONAL TECHNICAL DATA

ITALY	Ro 44	JULY
406		1943

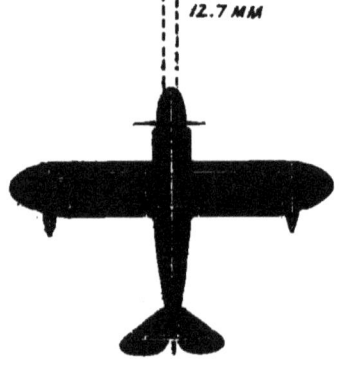 

Ro 44

DESCRIPTION

The Ro 44 is a floatplane that is probably in limited use by the I.A.F. "Ro" denotes Romeo, former manufacturer.

The aircraft is a single-engine, single-float biplane. Wings are of unequal span, designed to fold; top wing is the longer of the two. Top center section is "gulled" into the fuselage. Single-step central float is attached to fuselage by wire-braced struts. Stabilizing floats of wooden construction are inboard of the lower wing tips. Open cockpit is aft of top wing.

JULY 1943 — ITALY — 406

Ro 44

SINGLE-ENGINE FLOATPLANE

Mfr.: **MERIDIONALI** Crew: **ONE**
Duty: **FIGHTING**

PERFORMANCE

Max. speed **189** m.p.h. at **8,000** ft. altitude; 182 mph at sea level.

Cruising speed: normal **163** m.p.h.; economical **105** m.p.h.; at **6,500** ft. altitude.

Climb: to **6,500** ft. altitude in **3.8** min. (normal load); in 4.1 min. (with max. load).

Fuel: normal (est.) **75** U.S. gals.; max. **113** U.S. gals.

Service ceiling: normal load **26,000** ft.; max. bomb/fuel load **24,000** ft.; min. fuel/no bombs **28,000** ft.

RANGES

Speeds	With Normal Fuel/Bomb Load	With Max. Bomb Load	With Max. Fuel Load
Normal cruising	325 miles	miles	510 miles
Economical cruising	475 miles	miles	760 miles

POWER PLANT

Number of motors **1** Rated **700** horsepower each at **3,300** ft. altitude.

Description: **Piaggio "Stella" P.X RC., 9 cyl., air-cooled radial.**

Propellers: **3-blade, metal.**

Superchargers:

Misc.: **Long chord cowling.**

ARMAMENT

(F - fixed. M - free.)

For'd fuselage: **2 x 12.7mm (F)**
For'd wings:
Through hub:
Dorsal:
Lateral:
Ventral:
Tail:

BOMB/FREIGHT LOAD

Normal bomb load: _____ lbs.
Max. bomb load: _____ lbs.
Typical bomb stowage:
_____ lbs.
Alternate bomb stowage:
_____ lbs.
Freight and/or troops:
_____ lbs.

ARMOR

Frontal:
Windshield:
Pilot's seat:
Dorsal:
Lateral:
Ventral:
Bulkhead:
Engine:

SPECIFICATIONS

Materials: **Metal, wood, fabric.**

Span: **37'-11"** Length: **31'-10"** Height: **11'-6"** Wing Area: (gross) **358** sq.ft.

Weights: landing **4,400** lbs.; normal load **4,900** lbs.; max. load **5,150** lbs.

Misc.:

ADDITIONAL TECHNICAL DATA

Principal differences from the Ro 43 is that it is single-place instead of two-place and also caliber of armament is increased.

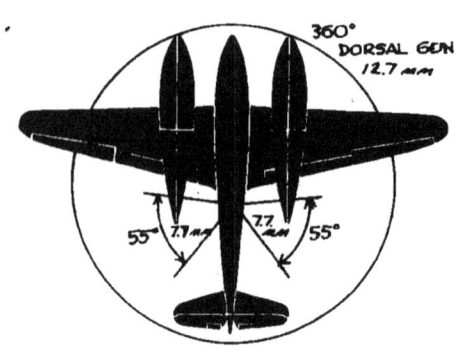
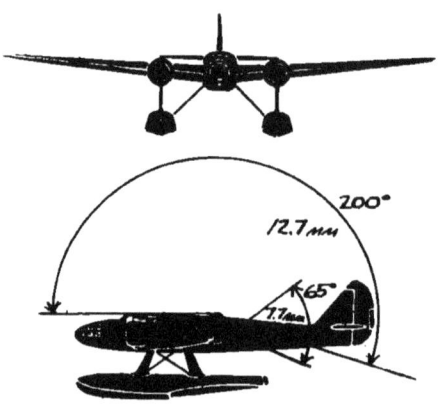

RS 14

DESCRIPTION

The RS 14 is a floatplane that is reported to be still in operation in limited numbers. "RS" denotes "Ricognicione Stiavelli" or reconnaissance aircraft designed by Stiavelli.

The aircraft is a twin-engine, twin-float mid-wing monoplane. Wings taper, more so on trailing edge than leading edge; tips are rounded. Camber-changing trailing edge flaps are fitted. Nose of fuselage is mainly transparent. Pilot's cockpit is forward of the leading edge. Twin metal floats are carried on braced, strutted assemblies.

JULY 1943		ITALY
	RS 14	407

TWIN-ENGINE FLOATPLANE

Mfr.: **FIAT.**   Crew: **PROBABLY THREE.**

Duty: **TORPEDO DROPPING. BOMBING. RECONNAISSANCE.**

PERFORMANCE

Max. speed __237__ m.p.h. at __13,000__ ft. altitude; 212 mph at sea level. (est.)

Cruising speed: normal __204__ m.p.h.; economical __150__ m.p.h.; at __13,000__ ft. altitude.(est.)

Climb: to __13,000__ ft. altitude in __10__ min. (est.)

Fuel: normal(est.) 542 U.S. gals.; max. _____ U.S. gals.

Service ceiling: normal load __27,000__ ft.; max. bomb/fuel load __30,000__ ft.; min. fuel/no bombs _____ ft.
              (est.)   (est.)

RANGES

Speeds	With Normal Fuel/Bomb Load	With Max. Bomb Load	With Max. Fuel Load
Normal cruising	(est.) 1,170 miles	_____ miles	_____ miles
Economical cruising	(est.) 1,450 miles	_____ miles	_____ miles

POWER PLANT

Number of motors __2__   Rated __840__ horsepower each at __12,500__ ft. altitude.

Description: __Fiat A.74 RC.38, 14 cyl., twin-row, air-cooled radial.__

Propellers: __3-blade, metal, constant speed, Fiat-Hamilton.__

Superchargers: _____

Misc.: __Long chord cowlings with controllable gills.__

ARMAMENT
(F - fixed. M - free.)

For'd fuselage: 1/2 m.g.'s probably
For'd wings: _____
Through hub: _____
Dorsal: 1 x 12.7 mm (M)
Lateral: 2 x 7.7 mm (M)
Ventral: _____
Tail: _____

BOMB/FREIGHT LOAD

Normal bomb load: __880__ lbs.
Max. bomb load: (est.) __1,760__ lbs.
Typical bomb stowage: _____
               __4 x 220__ lbs.
Alternate bomb stowage:

(est.) 1 Torpedo, __1,760__ lbs.
Freight and/or troops: _____ lbs.

ARMOR

Frontal: _____
Windshield: _____
Pilot's seat: _____
Dorsal: _____
Lateral: _____
Ventral: _____
Bulkhead: _____
Engine: _____

SPECIFICATIONS

Materials: __Metal stressed skin.__

Span: __64'-3"__   Length: __45'-6"__   Height: __17'-9"__   Wing Area (gross) 555 sq.ft.

Weights: landing (est.) 13,900 lbs.; normal load (est.) 16,000 lbs.; max. load _____ lbs.

Misc.: __Wing and fuselage of metal, stressed skin construction.__

ADDITIONAL TECHNICAL DATA

Dorsal gun in turret, probably power-driven.

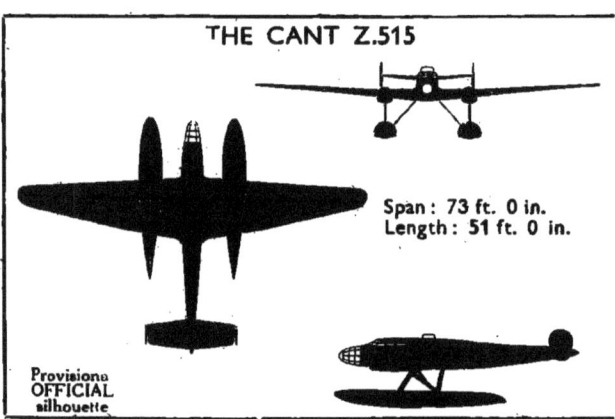

TYPE.—Multi-seat general reconnaissance floatplane.
MOTORS.—Two 750 h.p. Isotta Fraschini Delta R.C. 351-5 motors.
REMARKS.—The Cant Z.515 does not appear to be developed from any previous Cant designs and is in the same class as the Fiat R.S.14. Prominent features are its high aspect ratio mainplane, long slim fuselage, dihedral tailplane and twin outrigged fins and rudders of unusual shape. A power-operated dorsal turret is apparently fitted.

408

Mfr.:_____ Crew:_____
Duty:_____

PERFORMANCE

Max. speed_____ m.p.h. at_____ ft. altitude.
Cruising speed: normal_____ m.p.h.; economical_____ m.p.h.; at_____ ft. altitude.
Climb: to_____ ft. altitude in_____ min._____
Fuel: normal_____ U.S. gals.; max._____ U.S. gals._____
Service ceiling: normal load_____ ft.; max. bomb/fuel load_____ ft.; min. fuel/no bombs_____ ft.

RANGES

Speeds	With Normal Fuel/Bomb Load	With Max. Bomb Load	With Max. Fuel Load
Normal cruising	_____ miles	_____ miles	_____ miles
Economical cruising	_____ miles	_____ miles	_____ miles

POWER PLANT

Number of motors_____ Rated_____ horsepower each at_____ ft. altitude.
Description:_____
Propellers:_____
Superchargers:_____
Misc.:_____

ARMAMENT
(F - fixed. M - free.)
For'd fuselage:_____
For'd wings:_____
Through hub:_____
Dorsal:_____
Lateral:_____
Ventral:_____
Tail:_____

BOMB/FREIGHT LOAD
Normal bomb load:_____ lbs.
Max. bomb load:_____ lbs.
Typical bomb stowage:_____
_____ lbs.
Alternate bomb stowage:
_____ lbs.
Freight and/or troops:
_____ lbs.

ARMOR
Frontal:_____
Windshield:_____
Pilot's seat:_____
Dorsal:_____
Lateral:_____
Ventral:_____
Bulkhead:_____
Engine:_____

SPECIFICATIONS

Materials:_____
Span:_____ Length:_____ Height:_____ Wing Area:_____
Weights: landing_____ lbs.; normal load_____ lbs.; max. load_____ lbs.
Misc.:_____

ADDITIONAL TECHNICAL DATA

_____
_____
_____

3-7114, IP

U. S. GOVERNMENT PRINTING OFFICE: 1943 O - 542553